T0149990

THE BABY
IN THE BAG

Edited by

Hafza Girdap

Published by Blue Dome Press
335 Clifton Ave.
Clifton, NJ, 07011, USA
www.bluedomepress.com

Hardcover 978-1-68206-027-8
Ebook 978-1-68206-532-7

Library of Congress Cataloging-in-Publication Data
Names: Girdap, Hafza, editor.
Title: The baby in the bag / edited by Hafza Girdap.
Description: Clifton, NJ : Blue Dome Press, 2020.
Identifiers: LCCN 2020033704 (print) | LCCN 2020033705 (ebook) | ISBN 9781682060278 (hardcover) | ISBN 9781682065327 (ebook)
Subjects: LCSH: Political violence--Turkey. | Political persecution--Turkey. | Political refugees--Turkey--Biography. | Turkey--History----Coup d'état, 2016. | Turkey--Politics and government--21st century.
Classification: LCC HN656.5.Z9 V526 2020 (print) | LCC HN656.5.Z9 (ebook) | DDC 303.609561--dc23
LC record available at https://lccn.loc.gov/2020033704
LC ebook record available at https://lccn.loc.gov/2020033705

Contents

Editor's note

After the alleged coup attempt on July 15, 2016, tens of thousands of people have been dismissed from their jobs and many of them have been arrested on the grounds that they were members of the Hizmet Movement, a grassroots movement that emphasizes tolerance, interfaith dialogue, and education. These people have little to no hope to survive in this grueling atmosphere in Turkey and, as they are banned to travel, they have no other choice but flee the country by crossing the borders via dangerous routes at the risk of losing their lives. Many have not survived this journey to freedom, drowned in the Mediterranean, or successfully made it out but still remain separated from their families.

The following accounts are based upon true stories, however names and places have been changed for the safety of the victims' families.

We would like to thank everyone who has contributed to this book. Our sole wish is that the injustice, lawlessness, and victimization that many have been suffering from will come to an end as soon as possible via the reestablishment of rule of law.

About the Hizmet Movement

Hizmet is a transnational civil society initiative that advocates for the ideals of human rights, equal opportunity, democracy, non-violence, and the emphatic acceptance of religious and cultural diversity. It began in Turkey as a grassroots community in the 1970s in the context of social challenges being faced at the time: violent conflict among ideologically and politically driven youth, desperate economic conditions, and decades of state-imposed ideology of discrimination which mandated a particular lifestyle.

Over the years, Hizmet has transformed from a grassroots community in Turkey to a wider global effort with participants from all walks of life. Their work is centered upon, promoting philanthropy and community service, investing in education in order to cultivate virtuous individuals, organizing intercultural and interfaith dialogue events to promote a more peaceful coexistence.

Hizmet participants are inspired by the ideas and example of Fethullah Gülen, a Muslim scholar who has expressed the belief that serving fellow humans is serving God.

For more information: www.afsv.org

Editor's note on AST and APH Project

APH Project – The Project of Recording and Documenting the Persecution of Hizmet Movement

Advocates of Silenced Turkey (AST) is a non-governmental organization that runs its activities on a voluntary basis. The aim of AST is to bring before international public opinion the human rights violations including torture and the unlawful court trials and proceedings, which have been encountered in Turkey for the last two years. After the coup attempt of July 15, 2016, more than 160,000 innocent people lost their jobs in both the public and private sectors, with accusations and unjust convictions of being connected with the coup attempt. The State of Emergency, which was announced on July 20, 2016, gave the state unchecked authority in the disguise of combatting terrorism to persecute thousands without accountability and to undermine the fundamental principles of a democratic society and the most basic principles of universal human rights and values such as freedom of expression and freedom of press. Today, tens of thousands of highly qualified professionals including military officers, members of the judiciary, doctors, teachers, journalists, and academics, and more than 16,000 women and nearly 900 children, have been detained and imprisoned in Turkey for bogus terrorism charges.

As Advocates of Silenced Turkey, we engage in a number of activities in order not to keep silent about the injustices that have been taking place in in Turkey where rule of law has been suspended for a long time.

The project of recording and documenting the testimonies of victims aims to shed light on the injustices suffered by thousands of people in Turkey. Our volunteers have conducted hundreds of interviews and, thanks to their efforts, the victimizations and hardships that the victims experienced are now being recorded in both spoken and written formats. The main purpose of this project is to ensure that these tragic stories are not allowed to fade into oblivion and recorded accurately and impartially to leave firsthand sources for future generations. We also aim to bring this persecution to the attention of academics, media organizations, human rights associations, prominent community leaders and government representatives at the international level.

Each story in this book is the compilation of real-life stories encountered by real victims whose real names and details of events have not been revealed for the safety of their families in Turkey. We would like to thank everyone who made tireless and valuable contributions to this work. We wish Turkey will soon transform to a democratic society in which fundamental values like universal human rights and rule of law are duly observed.

Preface

How enchanting are you, o visage of freedom,
We are free of captivity, yet captivated by your love.
Namık Kemal

We are all travelers towards an unknown... We've fallen in love with an ideal that gives a promise of the eternal. An ideal that will reveal the unknown and enlighten the uncertain... An ideal that is sacred like the bread, valued like a promise, indispensable like freedom.

Every person is on a journey that is unique to themselves... But an ideal that is so great, a dream that is so boundless brings with it a journey that is far from easy. It brings with it a path that is ridden with deep pitfalls... A journey that is washed with floods and blocked by avalanches... A journey with no refreshing breeze... A path that is ruled by thunderstorms...

In the middle of this endless wilderness, we have no choice but to keep on moving forward... be it on foot... even barefoot maybe... walking over burning sand...

Be it on horse... bareback and unsaddled maybe... we have no choice but to gallop on, day and night, until we reach our destination...

Be it by plane... all alone, with no mother, no father by our side maybe... we have no choice but to cross over countries and continents, doing our best to hide our tears...

Be it inside a travel bag... uncomfortable as it may be... we have no choice but to cross over borders with the hushed silence of a baby, oblivious to all that is happening around us, just so that we may be able to say, "Yes, the world is my home."

Roads turn into more roads... minutes turn into hours... lives grow old... yet the state of a traveler, the nature of a voyager does not change. Ever so real, ever so fresh, just like the first day...

Each one of us holds a special role in this "journey" scenario... Be it by force, or by favor, we all take up our positions on the stage of life.

Heroes of the stories in this book were given the role to walk a rainy stage, on a snowy path against the bitter wind. With the strength they gathered from being a mother or father, from being individuals with dignity, they were able to do justice to and make the most of her scene. They are now on the verge of yet another tough journey as they set out to enlighten the "uncertain" lying ahead...

1

The Baby in the Bag

Dr. Rana

Hardworking and smart, I was the only child of a low-income Anatolian family. My father, even as he struggled to make ends meet with the salary of a civil servant, was nonetheless very supportive of my ideals of receiving an education. I attended a High School of Sciences where I was a boarding student. Then, I moved on to attend one of the most prestigious schools of medicine in Turkey. I was able to complete my education thanks to the scholarships that I had been awarded while staying in a dormitory, as well as the great sacrifices my family endured for my sake despite their already limited means.

I was introduced to the Hizmet Movement when I was at university. During those years, I volunteered to tutor and mentor high school students. Later on, during the time I was working as an assistant at the university, I would do my best to be supportive and helpful for the next generations who were going down the same path that I had previously traveled.

I met my future husband two years before graduation. He had also devoted himself to the Hizmet Movement, however, we had not been introduced to each other through the Movement. We were actually both students in the same department and our paths ended up crossing at one point. Right after graduation, my husband (who, at the time, was my fiancé) went back to his hometown for mandatory military service. At that point I also decided to go back to my hometown for a bit since I had been away from my family for years. I wanted to live with my family for a while and feel their presence close by me.

Two years later, after my husband-to-be had selected his specialty and settled in Ankara, we got married. The same year, I started my PhD studies in September 2011. Though my husband and I were both part of an academic circle of, I can say that we were far from working with the genuinely intellectual people that we would have expected. People would smile to each other and greet one another when met face to face but would start gossiping about one another the minute they turned their backs. They would also argue over the most basic things. This prompted us to keep our distance from them and to also remain quiet about our love for the Hizmet Movement. As a matter of fact, the pressure the government would shortly start to place on Hizmet people later proved how wise our decision had been. We continually distanced ourselves from others even more as pressure increased over time.

I had a very close friend, named Fidan, who was also married. Fidan and her husband were the only couple we would meet with on a regular basis. They were doctors like us, and we shared the same thoughts and feelings about the Hizmet Movement and, interestingly, had both gotten married around the same time. We were both trying to conceive a child and were receiving medical care to assist with conception. It seemed as if we were companions in a shared destiny. Unknown to us at the time, our destinies would become very shared in the near, and very dark, future.

The coup that changed everything

On July 15th, 2016, there was a coup attempt in Turkey. The government immediately blamed the Hizmet Movement and its volunteers. However, the coup took place right after Eid and, like all regular citizens, the people who were being accused of staging the coup were either away visiting family in their hometowns or – like us – on vacation. No one even bothered asking the question "Well, if these people were truly planning on staging a coup, why didn't they stay in the cities they lived in and take active part in carrying out the planned coup?" The accusations were without any sort of factual basis.

It was precisely during this time that my husband and I were vacationing at a hotel in a coastal town on the Mediterranean. We were scheduled to return to Ankara the next day to go back to our jobs, and we were hanging out chatting in the hotel lobby, enjoying our last night of vacation. I remember the television running in the background, but we were so immersed in our own conversation that we weren't even paying attention to what was on... We had no idea as to what was happening until 11 o'clock that night when we received a phone call from a friend in Ankara. As we spoke on the phone, there was the sound of jet fighters in the background coming from her end of the phone. Interestingly, she too hadn't heard anything about the coup attempt. As we continued to converse, the sounds got louder and louder. Confused, we finally had to hang up because we couldn't hear each other over the noise.

We started getting really worried and feared that something serious was happening. We turned around to tune in to the television behind us. The TV channels were talking about something related to a coup; there were jets racing through the skies, there was some news about the Parliament building being bombed – personally, as God is my witness – I worryingly thought to myself, "I bet it's some dispute with some foreign country and they've opened fire." After a while, because we were going to be hitting the road early the next morning, we went up to our room to get some sleep.

We drove back to Ankara the following morning; however, we could only enter the city via alternate routes since the government had blocked off all the main roads. Of course, we were still not fully aware of the gravity of the situation. We were, however, going to become quite aware a couple of days later when we returned to work. On my first day back, my PhD professor received a notice for his dismissal. I cannot forget that day when an armful of yellow envelopes arrived at the department. The people whose names were written on those envelopes learned later that they had just been suspended. Eventually, all those individuals were dismissed from their jobs. This incident shook our department like a bomb.

"Serves him right!" the people remarked about my professor after he had been sent away. Whereas just prior to him being taken away like that, he had been loved and respected by all, known throughout the department to be a professor who did his job well, a man who everyone wanted to work with. Like I mentioned before, our department was full of characterless individuals that started gossiping about him before he even had a chance to exit the room. In the following days, there was an air of distrust hanging over our department, and tensions kept increasing by the minute as everyone looked at one another with suspicion, viewing each other as potential informants. In fact, professors from other departments were even sending their assistants over to me to try and pry out any kind of information that they could.

Being made to pay the price for the coup!

The following year passed by with us watching in desperation as scores of innocent Hizmet Movement members were arrested one by one, killed through torture, and left to suffer through dire conditions physically, financially, and psychologically. Nevertheless, our own lives trudged on, and even though we were upset and dispirited, we kept going to work and doing our jobs as was necessary. The gravity of 2016 turned out to be a preview, however, of how tough the coming year was going to be.

Despite everything, 2017 did bring us something beautiful – our first baby. It was the beginning of August when our baby came into this world. The treatments had proved fruitful, and our Lord had, in the end, blessed us with a child. As happy as I was about this, a part of me was very upset for my friend Fidan. She had gone through the same treatments as us and was not able to bear any children.

I was more or less over the initial postpartum exhaustion by the time our baby was 40 days old and I thought it would be a good idea to introduce our family to our new baby. And so we traveled to our hometown where we visited with family for a couple of days. Afterwards, my husband went back to Ankara for his job while the baby and I stayed behind for a while longer. That was our initial plan, at least.

At home, we had a note by our front door that read: "Attention! Our baby is sleeping, please do not ring the doorbell." This meant that our doorbell had not been rung since our baby arrived. However, the morning after my husband made it back home, he was awakened by the endless ringing of our doorbell, which to him was quite a shock. He was shocked again to notice a group of police officers asking for my whereabouts when he opened the door!

Being arrested is one thing, but even just the fact that your home is raided by police and searched inside out is in itself so offensive and embarrassing. Just imagine, complete strangers come in and pillage every single corner of your private residence without showing any respect to your privacy and accuse you for actions you did not commit. Thank God that at least when my husband excused himself to go into the study to get dressed, he was able to think to hide away our passports.

There was a lady we attended religious study circles with, and, who knows, maybe it was because she was forced into it and maybe she felt she had no other choice — I don't know what the reason was — but it was her that reported me and my close friend Fidan to the police. My husband didn't tell me about this at the time, but he had spoken about it to my mother. But, he did call me up to say, "If for some reason they issue a search warrant for you, you need to give power of attorney to a lawyer ahead of time, just in case." He thought he had come up with a plan in case I were to get caught, but how was he to know that this would also be the plan that would drive me right into trouble.

I hadn't quite understood why my husband was asking me to get a power-of-attorney. We were already feeling suffocated by the country's current agenda, and we were making preparations to exit the country – legally – in the near future, so why the sudden need for a power-of-attorney now? Still, I did not insist otherwise, and my mother and I found ourselves at the notary. We went to the notary for a quick power-of-attorney procedure, however the process ended up becoming very odd. They started asking me all sorts of irrelevant questions. I started thinking to myself, "Isn't this taking a bit too long? No, no, stop worrying for nothing. This is a comprehensive power-of-attorney you're going after, it's completely normal for it to take this long." Just then, the young gentleman standing next to me caught my attention. I turned towards him, and we made eye contact. "Are you Mrs. Rana?" he asked. "Yes, but..," I started saying... as his cold words cut me off. "There is a search warrant for you. I have orders to take you away." I froze — I had absolutely no idea how I should respond. For a split second, I looked behind me towards the door, and there stood a group of civil police who had come to take me. The young police officer started interrogating me as we stood there: "Why do you think there is a search warrant for you?" "I have no idea" I said. "I've never had any problems with anyone to this day." Just at that moment, one of the assistants at the university hospital crossed my mind. After my professor was dismissed, she was constantly picking on me. She grilled, pressured, and harassed me many times and mockingly asked things like, "Admit it, are you one of them? Are you a FETO member?!"

My baby was crying incessantly while the police stood there waiting to take me in. My mother was looking around with terror in her eyes, and the people standing nearby were watching us with curiosity. I was in a state of indescribable and absolute shock. I had no choice but to do as I was told.

Because the report had been issued in Ankara, they told me that my testimony would be taken by the public prosecutor there. However, because the prosecutor did not accept SEG-BIS teleconference (Audio-Visual Information System), it was decided that I would be physically transferred to Ankara. My husband and my mother were there to accompany me – that is, they followed behind the police car that was taking me. There were three police officers, one of which was a woman. The local prosecutor was, thanks to God, conscientious enough to let me ride without being cuffed. In fact, he had even given the orders, "Let her nurse her baby whenever she wishes to."

It was a three-and-a-half-hour drive to Ankara, and I was being taken in a vehicle which traveled with no consideration of the traffic codes whatsoever. I was constantly looking back to see the car that my husband was following us in. So long as I could see him coming behind us, I felt I was safe.

We stopped once to nurse my baby. We were now pretty close to Ankara when we stopped at a nearby rest area and the police told me to eat something. They were probably thinking that I should eat and not be hungry in case I was arrested later on. My husband and I sat at a table while they sat at another table close by.

My husband was trying to comfort me, but I could see the terror in his eyes. "Don't be upset," he said. "We have the law and justice on our side, you have a tiny baby, they won't arrest you." He told me he would get a lawyer and that I needn't worry. Even as he was telling me not to worry, he was so worried himself that I couldn't relax either. He was speaking to me as though we were bidding farewell. As we got back on the road, I thought of checking my phone. I had considered leaving it at home, but the prosecutor and the police officers had told me to make sure that I carried it with me. Quite possibly they figured the prosecutor in Ankara would take hold of it for examination. I had a very close friend who had learned from my mother that I had been taken into custody, and that we were on the road. She started sending WhatsApp messages to me and deleted it when she figured I had read it. First she wrote, "Don't worry, all this will pass." Then she wrote, "Go back to the factory settings!" That's when the penny dropped. They were going to put my phone in for examination and, judging by the fact that I was being held under custody even when I had done absolutely nothing wrong, they could very well also concoct some kind of crime from even the most insignificant message they were to find. I immediately did what she told me and reset the phone to its factory settings.

Psychological torment

Sometime before being taken into custody, I had a very eerie dream: I passed through a deserted area with no buildings or people until I eventually came upon, and entered, a gray building. Inside, everything had a reddish tone to it, I climbed a narrow set of stairs, and I half opened the door to a room. I saw sacrificial meat inside the room. At the time I had the dream, I had tried hard to find a positive meaning from the dream, but it was now that the meaning of the dream seemed much more clear to me. Perhaps, through this dream, my Lord had shown me the hundreds of victims, who resembled the sacrifices, that had been locked up in those gray judicial buildings.

When I saw the military building (yes, I had been brought to the military quarters instead of the police station) that I was being delivered to by the police, a shiver ran down my spine. This building looked so much like the building I saw in my dream! As I was being escorted up similar looking stairs and into a room, I can't say that I didn't half expect that there would be sacrificial meat hanging down from the ceiling.

It was almost midnight when the commander on call greeted us when we arrived; he was a polite man. In fact, he told me I could bring my baby with me and that they had pre-pared a special place for the baby. For a second, I acted pretty naively and fell for his fake kindness, and called my husband to ask him what should we do. Thank God, he acted with a more sound mind and pretty much said to me, "Don't be absurd!" Of course he was right, but this was the first time I would be sep-arated from my baby, and I felt uneasy and upset. I had merely thought, well, since the conditions are favorable, and they've already set up a spot, let my baby stay with me.

In a few minutes, I would see for myself how special the spot was that they had set up for us. A bed of concrete, a metal toilet, a space barely ten square feet that was dark and reeked of sewage so intensely that you could feel your liver burning. Oh, and how that commander had pressured me, saying, "I can't let the baby in and out all the time; either the baby stays with you or doesn't come in at all." I decided to leave my baby with my husband. After I was locked up there, I was grateful that I hadn't brought in my baby with me. Either that commander did not have any children of his own or he just didn't have an ounce of compassion in him.

They emptied out my pockets and took away my phone, personal belongings, and even my shoe laces. I was escorted down that narrow staircase and into that tiny dark place, as if I were being placed in my grave. Countless number of prison cells were placed next to one another. As I was passing by, I caught a glimpse of who was in the first detention room – my dear friend Fidan. They had gotten hold of her before they'd come to me and had already locked her up. She probably saw me passing through, but she didn't even look up at me. No greeting, no looking up, not even a nod. This was yet another upsetting blow to me.

Night was just beginning as my iron door closed off my cell. Everything here was bad, but the worst part was the fact that there was no clock anywhere. There was a digital clock hanging above but the time it displayed didn't make any sense. Eventually that clock stopped working altogether, and when it did it felt like time had come to a complete halt. It was a tight space that felt like a grave as though we had been locked up in there to remain with our own selves and reflect.

I sat... I stood... I paced... I lay down... What felt to me like centuries going by was probably just ten minutes. What's more, as the hours stretched on, another problem arose. Being that I was a mother who had newly given birth and had been nursing, my breasts started to become swollen and I was in great pain. If they could at least give me some pain relievers, if only my pain could be quieted down somewhat... I called out, I yelled... Nobody answered my calls. I made foolish hand gestures towards the camera waiting for someone to notice, but still no one came. Finally, I heard a faint voice, both familiar and different. It was my friend in the detention room next to me, she was speaking in an icy tone so as not to give away our relationship. She said to me, "There's a red button there, you need to push that!" I did as she told me. I pressed and pressed the button countless times but no one came. I was up all night until the next morning, trembling with pain. I had to express my milk into the filthy toilet, the milk dripping all over my clothes... "At least give me a napkin!" I whimpered. "Please anybody, somebody help me please!" My throat had dried up from all the calls and screams... Helpless and exhausted, I asked for a drop of water, but still no one came. Left with no other choice, I drank the filthy water from the toilet.

I do not know how I made it through the night and saw the morning but somehow I did. It wasn't the early morning hours, maybe more towards noon, when finally the sun shone down on my detention room. A soldier carrying a red car seat brought me my baby. It felt like I hadn't seen my baby in months. I jumped up and caught hold of the car seat and hugged my baby, kissing him, smelling him, taking him all in. And of course I nursed him. My baby wasn't even two months old yet, he was just learning to smile and he smiled up at me and I smiled back. I spoke to him and said, "You, my precious baby, do not belong here... I promise you, we are going to get out of here, we will be free and we will never have to leave one another." He smiled as though he understood me, and I smiled back even more.

By the time I changed, nursed, and talked to my baby it had been over an hour already, and because I couldn't allow my baby to be in those filthy conditions any longer, I pressed the red button and called for the soldier to come and take him back. As the soldier took my baby away, I couldn't stop the tears from rolling down my cheeks. This separation was just too much to bear.

I learned later on that it was my mother and brother-in-law who had brought the baby to me, not my husband. The officials had insistently been asking him over and over, "You will be coming tomorrow, is that right?" And so, afraid that they would also take him, he decided not to come.

Not long after I parted with my baby they took me to a hospital and then over to the police station for me to give a statement. While I was giving my statement they asked me so many questions and made all kinds of accusations. Of course, I did not accept any of those accusations. Afterwards, I was shown a catalog full of pictures and was asked which of the individuals that I had been shown I personally knew. "None of them," I replied. Indeed, I did not know any of the individuals I was shown. Was I tensed up as I was being questioned? No. I had been through such a lonely and terrible night that, to be honest, I was just happy to be outside again and to be able to have a conversation with another human being, even if it was just to give a statement.

The lawyer my husband hired was also there with me. He tried to comfort me, "Don't worry," he said, "I will do everything I possibly can. You will make it out of this hole and, God-willing, you will go someplace far away and you will be free." I desperately needed to hear such words. Unfortunately, though, they ended up taking me back to that small and dark place once again.

The head games continue

I cannot imagine how people could endure this for days, months, even years, because I was certainly about to lose my mind. How was I going to make it to the morning in this hole! Interrupting my thoughts just then, a soldier came to take me away. Even though I had already given my official testimony, I was being taken again – this time to give another, unofficial testimony.

Waiting for me in the interrogation room was a commander along with a well-dressed man who introduced himself as Anil. I figured out later on that this man was an expert trained in the psychology of persuasion. It was possible to observe that this man, despite his calmness and friendly demeanor, was not my friend. He started a conversation in order to learn more about me, but most importantly to understand me better in order to find a way to make me confess to a crime that I did not commit. "So, your father was a poor man, sending you to school despite his limited means. Your father must've gone through some pretty difficult times just so you could receive an education, isn't that right? You are an intelligent young woman; you don't deserve to be here... You also have a small baby, don't you?" Supposedly, he also had a small baby girl of his own. He told me that once, when he was out on assignment, he had had to be away from her for days and lamented, "Oh, how difficult it had been." And what about me? What on earth would I do without my baby, all cooped up in this tiny hole? Let's say I brought my baby here with me, was a prison ward the best place to raise a tiny baby? How could a smart woman like me to do that to her baby? In short, the man was using my motherhood as a weapon against me to try and get me to "confess." He finished off his words with this sentence: "You can't take offence at the government, it is never too late to make amends. Confess to what you know, save yourself!"

Being a doctor, I also had received education on "Psychology and Body Language," and I could easily figure out what this man was trying to do. I chose not to resist; I listened to what he had to say until the very end. I knew very well that anything I were to say would be used as evidence against me. Also, rather than going back into that dark cell, I saw no harm in extending the conversation a bit more. Naturally, he saw my silence as concession and figured he was on the right track. He continued to "sweet talk" me for about an hour and a half. When he was done talking, he finally spilled the beans, saying, "How about we send for your attorney, would you like to go over your testimony once again?"

Again, rather than having to go back into that dark cell, I chose the option to chat with my lawyer for a while. I accepted the offer. While he was enjoying the notion that he had won me over, I, on the other hand, was happy to have the chance to meet once more with my lawyer. When my lawyer was called to come in the evening he got a bit anxious thinking that I accepted to become an informant; when he realized what was really going on, though, he was relieved. He personally didn't have any connection with the Hizmet Movement; however, he was greatly bothered by all the injustice being committed. "You have a strong case," he told me. "Your baby is so little, at least they will postpone your trial, release you with a pending trial. This will buy you some time to be able to make it out of the country. "

A short while later, I was taken in to be interrogated once again. My lawyer advised me: "Do not say anything! Just start crying and say, 'I don't know anything, I only want to be with my baby.' Cry out, 'I beg of you, please bring my baby, I miss him so much!" Okay, but I couldn't possibly put on an act like that! "You don't need to put on an act anyway," he said. "Just think about the fact that you are being put in prison and being separated from your baby!"

And, indeed, like he said, I did not need to put on a show at all. Anil had already left, but this time, the commander came; the one who was in the room during the previous interrogation but didn't speak. The second I thought about my baby, I burst into tears. This one must have been more conscientious than the other because once I started crying, he did not insist on anything and let me be. It was Thursday night. I had a court hearing scheduled for the next day. In other words, it would be Friday, and if my testimony wasn't taken I would have to stay there over the weekend. Even the thought of it was driving me crazy.

In the morning, Fidan and I were both loaded into a vehicle. There were three other police officers aboard the vehicle, two in the front, one in the back. My closest friend and I had spent two days in the same hellish place, right next to each other, but we had barely spoken a word to one another. We did not talk then either, we simply exchanged the phrase "May this pass soon" like two strangers. We figured that the police officers were especially putting us together in order to encourage us to talk and figure out if we knew each other or not. We neither deliberately averted our eyes from one another, nor did we show any signs that we knew each other. We behaved in the same fashion any two newly acquainted individuals who had been detained for the same reasons would behave and converse.

We first went to the hospital. We dodged a possibly horrible accident by the skin of our teeth; the police officer was driving like crazy. We finally arrived at the courthouse. Interestingly, the police officers who had just a minute ago been chit-chatting with us on the drive over all of a sudden grew serious and slid handcuffs over our wrists. In all honesty, this wasn't something done to us specifically; anyone who was being arrested for the same ridiculous reasons was subjected to the same treatment. Such were the orders. The purpose was to both create an image that "these people are criminals/terrorists" and to also dishearten the close family members who were waiting with high hopes at the doors of the courthouse. And, without a doubt, they were fulfilling their purpose.

All doctors take the "Hippocratic Oath" before they start their profession. It is a vow to dedicate one's life to helping others live; and yet, at that very moment, I was sitting across from a prosecutor and being accused of having initiated a bloody coup attempt. As if that were not enough, that prosecutor, through "the power" given to him not by the law but by a political authority, was accusing me of "not being a good mother and not considering the well-being of my small baby." How could I ever do such a thing?! He was telling me that he too had a small baby and would do anything for her! I was subjected to these accusations for a whole ninety minutes. I calmly told him that I was in fact thinking about my baby, and that I was deeply upset and hurt. But I did not know anything regarding the information they were looking for and therefore did not have anything to tell him.

Interestingly, as my testimony was being taken, my attorney was there with me; however, he did not intervene at all. I learned the reason for that later on. My attorney's previous client had also been an innocent victim who was being detained for "FETO" accusations, and – under the Erdogan dictatorship – the act of "advocating" for us was itself considered a criminal act. Therefore, my attorney did not want to be seen as being too defensive on my behalf. Another reason was that right before the interrogation, he had been summoned by the prosecutor and been pressured to "push me into confession," and he was given no other choice than to say that he would do everything he could to make that happen. Thus, he was unable to back me up during the testimony.

I had been inside the prosecutor's office for an hour and a half straight, giving my testimony, and I was drained of all energy. Honestly, when I stepped out of the room I had practically no hope left of being released. The prosecutor's room was separated from the corridor by a glass screen; as we had stood in there waiting to give the testimony, I saw my father-in-law and brother-in-law down the hall looking in my direction. Naturally, wanting to avoid any possible arrests, my husband was not able to come. My brother-in-law was trying to make me smile from where he stood in the hallway, but I couldn't bring myself to even fake it. When I looked in their direction I tried to smile, and I tried to imagine I was exiting the building as a free woman, leaving with them and going home; but, as soon as I turned back, I would see the prosecutor and would come face to face with reality once again.

As I was waiting in front of the courtroom – under police supervision – with my brother-in-law and father-in-law, my dear friend Fidan came with her husband, and they also sat down to wait. At one point, I glanced over in their direction. They were chatting and laughing as though they had somehow sensed that she was going to be charged. It was as if they were, in a sense, saying goodbye to each other. At that moment, she appeared to have fully submitted herself to whatever was awaiting her, like she was saying, "Whatever comes from You, O Lord, I accept it with all my being." No doubt about it, I was not as strong as she was. Maybe it was because I had a small baby, and I was being overly sensitive, I don't know, but I felt in need of even just a small fraction of hope to keep me going.

As we stood there, the court personnel took off for their noon break. As the ushers were leaving, my attorney felt the need to walk up and ask, "What time will you resume?" The ushers took a look at me and asked, "Isn't yours the case that's being released?" As much as this statement gave us some hope, it also goes to show us exactly the despicable situation of justice in the country; even the ushers were somehow informed about the decision of a case well before the hearing was even held. The hearing did not even last ten minutes. I told the judge that I did not accept any of the accusations against me, and the moment I heard him say, "...shall be released under judicial control with no signature duty..." I have to admit I was relieved beyond words.

I was pleased, but was I bursting with happiness? Not so much, unfortunately. It was a very hollow joy because as I was leaving I witnessed my dear friend Fidan saying goodbye to her husband as she was being taken to prison. I later heard that her husband was also going to be arrested about a year later. When you're not able to be with your loved ones as you wish, even the most joyful times don't feel so joyful anymore.

My own wish, on the other hand, had come true – I was returning home with my brother-in-law and father-in-law; but there was a certain bitter sweetness to it. As we drove, we first passed by our old home, then the building which was now my "former" workplace, and the home I came into as a bride, the place where I spent the happiest days of my life. And oh, my workplace... how excited and happy I had been when I first started. We passed the place where I got coffee when I walked to work in the mornings. I remembered how I had taken refuge in that little shop as the rain started pouring on me one day. I came to realize how I had built a world around me, consisting of my social life and my career. Just as the world itself, all that "life" around me had been a fleeting lie. And now, here I was, riding along in a car, bidding farewell to it all through mournful, teary eyes.

Thank God I was free now, but there was no guarantee that we wouldn't be taken in the next day with another ridiculous accusation. That's why the only thing we wanted to do was to get out of Turkey. However, we did have one problem. My husband and I both had "Green Passports," which allows the bearer to travel visa-free to some countries. But they gave our baby a regular passport. Because of that, we couldn't travel to Europe without first getting him a visa. We thought, "If we go to the American Consulate, the Turkish police will be there and they will get suspicious." We couldn't go there, so we decided to make an application with the Canadian Consulate. My husband mailed out the documents that we had put together.

Meanwhile, my husband could not stay home with us out of fear of being arrested. My mother decided to stay with us since my baby and I were alone in the house. My husband was staying with a relative of his and could only come out secretly once in a while to come see us. I was scared out of my mind that someone would follow him and report him to the police. I was being filled in on all that was going on outside, through a visiting friend from work, and I was worried and anxious.

The more inclined we were to hurry things up and get away as soon as possible, the slower things seemed to move forward. It took nearly a month and a half for us to hear back from the Canadian Consulate, which ultimately resulted in a denial anyway. We had only one last resort left: leaving the country with the help of smugglers!

A mother's nightmare

We had previously contacted the smugglers and had found some people who would help us escape through Georgia. My mother, mother-in-law, and my husband's cousin joined us as we boarded a plane and flew into Trabzon, our first stop in our escape. It was in the very early hours of the day. Without wasting any time, we rented a car and drove to Hopa, a city in northeastern Turkey close to the Georgia border. From there, we were all together going to pass over to Georgia.

We arrived in Hopa around noon and somehow had to spend the rest of the day at a tea garden and a mosque while waiting for night to settle. We paced back and forth for hours with nothing to do and too anxious to be joyous or happy. We were already on edge, and to top it off the weather was cloudy, the sea was crashing with waves, and the rocky cliffs seemed to gloom over us, suffocating us even more so. It wasn't called the "Sarp (meaning steep) Border" for nothing.

Time stood still. The hours seemed to go on forever. Emotionally, none of us were in the "we are going away for real" state. We were feeling incredibly tense and there was a "let's just get this over with as best as we can" feeling in the air. Finally, it was time to go. Each of us were allowed to take only one backpack so that it would look like we were tourists. There was a tremendous stress weighing down on each one of us. We grew even more tense by the minute as the guides gave us directives with stone cold, serious expressions.

We were just about to head out when one of the smugglers dropped an unexpected bomb on us: that we had to hide the baby! He gave us a travel bag and told us to put the baby in it. "Absolutely not!" I objected. My mind started immediately racing, and I didn't believe there was any way he could survive considering how tiny he was. I was certain that he would suffocate. To my dismay the smuggler said, "You have no other choice! Either you do what we say or you forget the whole thing!"

What an incredibly difficult decision this was for us to make – especially for me, his mother. What if he cried?! What if he couldn't breathe?! What if he suffocated?! We were going through this horrific adventure for his sake, and if we were to just lose him like that then what would be the point?! On the other hand, we had come all this way and gone through all this trouble and now deciding to not go through with it would mean that we were ready to accept all the possible outcomes that would come with that decision. Within seconds so many scenarios ran through my head: "If I end up in prison, how will I be able to raise my baby? Either he'll be deprived of sunlight and fresh air or we'll have to be separated for God knows how long. I won't be able to hear him say "mommy." I won't be able to watch him start crawling and take his first steps." We had no other choice – we were so incredibly desperate that we accepted the man's conditions, but we felt miserable beyond description. "How are we going to go about doing it?" we asked him. "You're going to sleep-drug the baby," he replied. At this moment, I completely lost whatever composure I had remaining within me and burst out saying, "What! He's too tiny to be given any drugs!" I couldn't keep a cool head anymore; the doctor side of me was gone, and the mother side of me had taken over. I was crying inconsolably. We thought about giving the baby the lightest drug possible which would not harm him, but we were so overwrought that our brains weren't operating. At last, I called up a doctor friend of mine and asked for advice.

My friend gave me the name of an allergy medicine for babies, one of its side effects was that it was sleep inducing. We went and bought the medicine but had no idea how much of it we should give the baby. We finally decided on giving him one unit and even ended up spilling half of it when giving it to the baby because our hands were shaking so hard. Fortunately, the baby finally fell asleep without much trouble, probably since he hadn't slept at all during the day with all the running around we did. We figured out later on that the dose we gave the baby had been too little and thus couldn't have produced any side effects, which meant that the baby had just naturally fallen asleep. He had slept because of exhaustion but we just didn't know that at the time. It's a good thing that we didn't.

The moment that we dreaded most had finally arrived, and it was now time to put the baby in the travel bag. No one could bring themselves to do it, we all wanted to pass the horrible task over to someone else. I was circling around the car, sobbing and crying, "We can't do this!" Neither myself nor my husband could work up the courage to put our son inside a bag, the vessel that could very well end up becoming his coffin.

It was too much to bear; I couldn't even look in that direction. At that moment, it was such a blessing that my mother was such a cool-headed woman; as I was crying outside the car, she calmly placed our baby in the travel bag. My chest was pounding so hard that I thought it would burst open.

It was time to pass through the border, and it was going to be the most difficult part yet. One of the smugglers said, "Let the mother carry the bag," but I couldn't bring myself to do it. On the one hand, as the baby's mother, I thought, "I am the one that can best tend to my baby." I didn't want to put him in anyone else's trust; yet, on the other hand, I couldn't keep calm. Seeing my meltdown, the man decided that my husband should carry the bag.

The cafe had long closed up, and all of a sudden, there were gypsies everywhere. They were all dressed in wide, loose clothing. We learned that they were carrying contraband underneath their clothes; in other words, they were smugglers. Because inspection was low during the night hours, they had picked this time frame to pass through.

My husband passed through first. As he proceeded with the handbag in his hands, we said prayers after him, but I couldn't sit still. My heart was pounding out of my chest. Every second felt like an eternity that was completely eclipsed by all of the horrible situations that could unfold in the following few minutes. My husband's cousin was trying to engage me in conversation and divert my attention, but my mind was fixed entirely on my baby. The two mothers were sitting in the back, crying, and I was with the cousin, pacing to and fro.

Finally, we received a call from my husband – they had made it through! Just as I was about to rejoice, a horrible scenario ran through my mind: "What if I can't make it through?! What if this was the last time I saw them both?!" I tried to calm myself down – I told myself that at least he's with his father. and they have their freedom; but still, a part of me was burning inside.

It was now my turn to pass. As I walked over towards security, I was still trying to calm myself down by telling myself, that I had to remain calm if I wanted to be reunited with my husband and my baby. I was trying to think about other things, happy thoughts and happy days to come. As my turn approached, I could feel my heart pounding in my throat. It was just like in the movies, everything and everyone around me had fallen silent; there was only a constant hum in the background.

Finally, the police officer was now looking over my passport. He could say, "Come with me to the office"; he could say, "Step over to the side"; he could say anything... But all he said was, "Go." Oh thank God, thank God! I walked and kept on going. I walked through a dark corridor and came out on the other end. And there was my husband, sitting with our baby in his arms. I cannot find the words to describe my joy at that moment. Afterwards, together, we walked over to the Georgian checkpoint. As we passed through, we were setting sail for a whole new life. Our mothers came after us.

Thus began the couple of months we would be spending in our neighbor country. The first thing we did was to check into a hotel. However, because the hotels there are generally used for "sinful" purposes, it was filthy beyond belief. And, supposedly, we had been set up with the cleanest hotel possible.

A stopover in Georgia

After staying for five days at the hotel in Batum, we went on to
Tbilisi where the American Consulate was located. We figured
that they could give us a visa immediately and then we would
be on our way. Unfortunately, things didn't go as planned.
Since our baby didn't have a Green Passport, we were unable to
enter into Europe. Because we didn't have a residency permit
in Georgia, the American Consulate wouldn't even schedule
an appointment for a visa interview. We had rented a home for
fifteen days, but it seemed like we were going to be stuck in this
country forever. We tried thinking of alternative ways of making it out. When we realized that it might take a bit longer to
find a way out of Georgia we decided to move to a new place in
a community where many Turkish people were already living.
In fact, there were a couple of other families living there that
were in transition just as we were. Meanwhile, we were still
trying to figure out a way to make it to any European country.
We paid some money to a lady who told us she was a travel
agent for visa to Lithuania, but we soon realized we had been
swindled when the money disappeared into thin air.

We refused to lose hope after enduring so much, and my
husband would check the American Consulate website every
single day, wishfully thinking, "Maybe we can at least get an appointment this time." It was mid-December, as I remember, and
it had been about a month and a half since we had crossed over
to Georgia. One evening, as usual, my husband popped on the
website to check. We were able to get in this time! We couldn't
believe our eyes! Without wasting a second, we made an urgent
request for a visa. It was a Tuesday, and they gave us an appointment for Thursday. We were both tense as we went to the

Consulate on the day of the interview, but the event invitation Harvard University had sent my husband was going to make everything easier. Thank God, at the end of the interview we were granted the visa!! Only those who have lived through the same experience can understand the kind of joy we felt that day.

Though we only stayed in Georgia for about a month and a half, we made great friends there. We were fifteen families now, and we all shared the same fate. We had bonded over our shared struggles in our homeland where we were accused of crimes that we did not commit. They were so happy for us when they heard that we had gotten our visas, but, of course, they were also so sad... these would be our final days in that country. Our last evening together with our friends was so wonderful and so full of sorrow at the same time. They had organized a mini farewell for us; everyone had cooked a dish and brought us gifts. Despite their limited means and the fact that they were all going through hard times, these beautiful and humble people had each brought us something special as a parting gift. We squeezed each one of those gifts into our suitcase to bring them with us, and to this day, we have them displayed in the most special part of our home. Those small but meaningful gifts will forever be cherished in our home to remind us of that time in our lives, a time of both hope and sorrow.

Our mothers were not going to be accompanying us any further on our journey, and thus it was time to see them off back to Turkey. As one could expect, this was an incredibly difficult thing to do. No matter how much they wished for us to seek our freedom, we had grown so attached to one another in this one-and-a-half-month period that we had been living together.

After they departed it was time for us to make it to our own flight. Everything was going smoothly up until check-in when we found ourselves face to face with the meaningless obstinacy of the officer there. The officer, whose only duty was to "check-in" the passengers, refused to let us board the plane! Supposedly, the reason was because others who had previously traveled from Georgia to Germany had applied for asylum there. Our flight to New York was with a stopover in Germany. We objected, saying, "How does this concern you? That's their problem, isn't it?" but the officer refused to listen. The man did not let us board the plane. He said he was going to get us a ticket to Istanbul instead. Another man who also carried a Green passport like us was held from boarding the plane as well. In the end, neither that person nor us were able to fly to Germany.

Though unable to board the German flight that morning at 5 am, we were somehow still able to buy a ticket to Ukraine and boarded the plane that same evening, exactly twelve hours later, at 5 pm. Well taken care of with the snacks that our new and forever friends in Georgia had packed for us, we had a four-hour flight and landed in Kiev. From there, with no more problems to hold us back, we connected to our other flight and flew to New York.

Finding our new home

Finally, we had landed in New York City's JFK Airport and reached our final destination, safe and sound. We stayed at a friend's house in New York for ten days, during which time we had the opportunity to think things through. We wondered if we should stay in the United States, or if we should move on upwards to Canada. We had a small baby and we did not have much savings. Whatever little we had, we had to use it wisely. We did our research and looked around. In the end, Canada seemed to make the most sense for us in terms of the conditions and opportunities. We had to make a decision and settle down as soon as we possibly could. We had friends who had previously made it over to Canada, so we spoke to them on the phone and asked for their advice. After listening to their experience, we were convinced that this would make the most sense for our family. We decided to cross the border into Canada and seek asylum there. We went to the border on a cold morning. We had an immense feeling of uneasiness weighing down on us with every step that we took forward. Our taxi driver must have sensed it, too, for he felt the need to comfort us. "Don't be afraid, and don't be shy. This is your God-given right," he said.

We got out of the taxi still feeling the same uneasiness. We had only taken a few steps when two police officers approached us. One of them, in fact, helped us carry our bags. We were trying to keep cool so they wouldn't notice anything out of the ordinary, or so we thought. But, as it turns out, they had already figured out why we were there as they escorted us inside.

Are you sure?

After we had been escorted inside a container-style police station type place – which was where the people seeking asylum were received – we were asked if we were certain that we wished to remain under custody and seek asylum. It hurt deep down to say it, to renounce our homeland and declare that we were fugitives. But it was our reality. This reality had been forced upon us by Erdogan's regime, whose tyranny scapegoated us and so many innocent people. We were forced out of our homeland, forced to go begging for democracy from another country, to go seeking our God-given right of freedom in other countries. This was the case, whether we liked it or not.

Our phones and all other belongings, except for the baby's, were taken from us and we had to wait a half hour as everything was searched and examined one by one. Afterwards, we boarded yellow buses – together with the other asylum seekers – and we were taken to another small police station. We waited for 4-5 hours inside another container building. I immediately remember that exact day whenever I experience any snowy or icy weather because of all the waiting I had to do that day. Because we had been the last to arrive, we ended up being the ones who waited there the longest. In the end, they took a testimony only from my husband and then we were transferred to another border police station. We were offered some food for the first time when we arrived there. After going hungry for so long, we gobbled up the applesauce and sandwich they gave us in a matter of seconds. We were asked if we wanted to call anyone, and of course we wanted to contact my mother and let her know that we were in Canada, a free country that promised to respect us and keep us safe. What followed afterwards were a set of routine procedures; fingerprints, photographs, signatures, and a whole lot of forms to fill out.

We had to spend the night there because the procedures took a long time. We were taken into a big room and made to wait. When it was nighttime the table and chairs were folded up and we were given blankets. Everyone had to sleep lying on the floor, but they did provide us with a portable bed for our baby. It was freezing cold throughout the night. As more and more asylum seekers came one after the other, the room kept on getting more crowded and the night we spent there turned out to be pretty rough.

So many different kinds of people were among us in that crowded room. People that had fled from war, persecution, fearful children, families whose fear and uncertainty could be read in their eyes. A feeling of relief and thoughts of, "I'm in a good place now;" and on the other hand, hearts trembling with worries of, "What now?" So many people in the same situation. I could understand what each of them were going through. I could understand because we were going through the same experience.

Towards noon the next day my husband and I were taken in separately to give our testimonies and, then once more we were boarded onto buses – this time on our way to Montreal. We were taken to a refugee shelter at the local YMCA.

A new life...

As I look back at those days now, I think to myself, "A whole year has passed by." It has now been a full year since we left behind our social status, families, property, assets, and of course the "terrorist" label that had been thrown on us, not to mention our pride and egos. We left it all behind and came to this new world.

And now, Canada had gifted us with a new baby, a little bit of hope but, naturally, a whole lot of difficulty. My husband, while delivering orders to make money, is also preparing for his exams in order to be able to start his Ph.D. studies at a university in the field of epidemiology. I, on the other hand, though it's definitely not my style, have settled at home as a homemaker and mother, and am raising my two children.

Life itself is a world of tests and no matter where you are, even though the situations may change, the fundamental characteristic stay pretty much the same. I think what's truly essential is being able to consent to your destiny. It's all a part of a Master Plan, is it not?

Right now we are unable to carry out our professions; our diplomas are accredited but that's not all there is to it. We have to pass certain exams, and the quotas are so limited. Each exam costs a substantial amount of money. I'm not complaining; rather, I'm merely describing our situation. In the end, the reason we came here was not to carry out our profession but to be able to live our lives as human beings and in peace. The notion of one day being able to return to our professions will continue to chatter on inside our hearts and minds, keeping us full of hope that one day it might be possible.

If someone were to ask me, "Have you been able to adapt?" I would answer, "I feel like we do not belong here." The conditions we find ourselves in make us feel that way, all the way to our core. From financial problems, to not being able to sufficiently express ourselves, to simply the fact of being a refugee in this country – all of these are things that wound a person's self-esteem.

"Would I want to return eventually?" Both yes, and no.

Yes, I would, because both my husband and I were successful individuals in our area of expertise. However, the slanders continue to label us like a piece of rot. I believe that one day justice will work its way into our country, and our careers and all that have been taken away from us will be returned once again. And so, I would want to return in order to be able to witness the cleansing of this dirt that's been thrown on us.

No, I would not like to return to Turkey, because the people who we idolized in our minds and hearts as being nearly
angel-like, describing them as "The People of Anatolia," after
seeing how judgmental and merciless they could be, even the
slightest thought of this kind of persecution recurring ever
again runs a chill down my spine. It absolutely terrifies me that
such evil could return one day, or that it even exists in the first
place. I hope and I pray that our fate holds a bright future for
us in our new country.

2

A Life of Adventure

Idil Sen

Finding love in an unlikely place

I cannot describe the day I met my would-be husband as the best day of my life; it was the most unpleasant day of my life. I met him at the funeral of my mother. My father had already passed away twenty years ago. While seeing my mother off to eternity and expecting God to show me and my siblings a way through our sorrow, I would meet my future husband.

I was a young and beautiful girl. The number of candidates who proposed to me was pretty high. But unfortunately, I was an orphan and this resulted in candidates changing their mind about marrying me, as it implied additional burdens on them for the rest of their lives. They were aware that if they married me, they also would have to take care of my younger sisters. Nobody wanted to take that responsibility on their shoulders. I heard confessions such as, "We really liked you and wanted our son to marry you, but because of your sisters, we changed our minds." No one dared to take such a responsibility, except for my husband. In the following years, he was going to consider them as his own sisters, support them both financially and emotionally, and not prevent me from taking care of them. My husband is compassionate and courageous, and these positive attributes of his would help us immensely to weather the coming storm.

I was a hairdresser. I was running a beauty salon and I did my job well. I was very busy both at home and at work.

I was introduced to the Hizmet Movement through my husband. My husband was a generous host and he loved inviting people over through his Hizmet connections. I had no problem entertaining guests who were visiting our home, for I knew my husband was a decent man. I did not have any problem with enrolling our kids in Hizmet affiliated schools either. After all, their success rates were very high and students were treated lovingly by their teachers. I would have sent them to better schools if they existed. Most of the educated and elite people in my city were sending their kids to these schools as well because the quality was undeniable.

The beginning of the end

July 15, 2016, began as any normal day typically begins. However, word rapidly spread in the evening that a coup d'etat was taking place in Istanbul. My husband was abroad and he called me to check out what was going on. My mother-in-law and sister-in-law were with us when we heard the news and immediately switched on the television. I was breastfeeding my newborn. We had no idea what was going on, but Istanbul's main bridge was blocked and there were tanks and soldiers in the streets. My father-in-law searched the TV channels and told us that we did not have to panic because he had witnessed military coups in the past and that it was clear to him that this was not a coup. We remained calm and blissfully ignorant of what was really about to unfold in the coming weeks, months, and years.

The AKP (Justice and Development Party) government, and especially Turkish President Recep Tayyip Erdoğan, quickly accused members of the Hizmet Movement as the masterminds behind the coup. He even went so far as to argue that we had been preparing for it for the past two and a half years. On the day of the coup I was not trying to overthrow the government; I was breastfeeding my child.

We hoped and prayed that the coup would come and go without any drastic change and that our lives would continue without change. But deep down, we knew that such a catastrophic event would not just blow over without repercussions. I was a hairdresser at the time and had to cautiously meet with the rest of my team and customers in the following days as our country was still in a state of confusion and insecurity.

Your passports are missing!

My husband was often travelling to other countries. We eventually ended up wanting to move abroad, however my pregnancy made it very difficult. I encouraged him to travel and find suitable countries for us to live in where we could work and be happy. If he found a place, I would move there, but if not, he would come back. I could not dare risk changing my life so drastically on so much uncertainty.

My husband had left the country in March, a few months before the coup attempt. In fact, he was a civil servant but since I just gave birth at that time, he used his paternal leave for two years and flew to the U.S. He had been planning to settle there and wanted to bring us as well. I had wanted the same, but was waiting for our baby to get a little older before making the journey and having to adjust living in a new country. But then, the coup attempt happened.

All the personal leaves of civil servants were canceled, including my husband's. He was also told to return to the country, however this did not make sense considering how much the situation was deteriorating. It made more sense for us to try and get to him in America. But we unfortunately had not applied for our American visas. Because of this situation, my husband told me to go to Germany and wait for the visa process there. There was nothing wrong with this because we went abroad many times, and since I had been attending many occupational workshops I had a Schengen Visa.

A short time later we bought tickets and went to the airport with my kids. There, the airport officials were going to confiscate our passports and shamelessly tell us that our passports were lost. I said, "How come they are lost? Here, I am holding them in my hand!" Because we were a well-known family in the city, people began to look at us. They began to approach us and tried to see what would happen. They took us from a room to another a couple of times and in the last room, they put a paper on the table which was stating that our passports were lost and they ordered us to sign it. I got mad and refused to sign it. I had left the country many times and there was no reason to deny my departure. I was holding them in my hand and showed the officer that they were not lost. All of a sudden he grabbed them and started tearing them. I had no choice but to sign the paper.

We ended up returning back home. I could not even comprehend what had just happened and was extremely upset. In the following days, the rumors and lies about what happened to us at the airport were going to spread more and more. This was going to make me even more sad to the point that I could not go to work for several days.

The harassment continues

I didn't leave the house due to my sorrow for a while. Then one morning, our doorbell rang. I covered my head with a scarf and as I half-opened the door, I saw many policemen standing there. I told them that my state of dress was not proper and that I would let them in the house if they would hold on a second. I was told not to shut the door and a female police officer entered my home and told me to get dressed.

The woman followed me into my bedroom and forced me to change in front of her without any privacy. My baby was crying loudly in the cradle and she did not even let me pick her up. But I insisted and moved to get my baby. Right when I turned towards the crib I noticed a Qur'anic prayer that was written in the cursive writing of Mr. Fethullah Gülen's, the scholar who inspired thousands of people in the Hizmet Movement, I grabbed it with a quick hand move, since I knew that this could be used as evidence against me. Then I told the lady officer that I had to go to the bathroom to change my baby's diaper. I needed to get rid of the paper or hide it, but since it was a Qur'anic verse and I wanted to respect it and I was not able to throw it away. Thus, I took it in my mouth, chewed it over and over, and swallowed it.

After that, the policewoman told me that she was going to leave, return, and wanted me to open the door when she rang the bell. She told me that they were going to enter my house, read our rights, and search the house. I was confused about what was going on but then I figured out that they had needed a staged show where they would videotape the operation.

As I opened the door again, they rushed into the house altogether, and they talked about my husband being a member of a terrorist organization, FETO (An abbreviation for a false terrorist organization) and they searched everywhere for any "evidence" of affiliation with Hizmet. After the coup attempt we had to throw all of our books away or get rid of them somehow since newspapers, CDs, and books were considered serious criminal evidence. We had to remove our books, which could fill half of a big truck. This was devastating to us since they were all valuable books of reference.

But some of them we somehow forgot to hide and the policemen could see what we had not been able to see. One sermon video of Mr. Gülen, one old Zaman newspaper copy, and a Sızıntı magazine. This was all the necessary evidence they needed to accuse us of being terrorists. Not weapons, pistols, or knives, but newspapers and magazines.

It is common Turkish tradition to treat all guests with respect and hospitality, no matter who they are. The search took hours, and while they were looking for evidence to prove that we were terrorists, I was serving them fruit, water, and juice. They were eating what we offered and while at the same time trying to prove that we were criminals. It was a tragic and comical scene. They were acting the opposite when the cameras were on. They were asking, "Did your husband go to religious gatherings, was he an active Hizmet member, did people from Hizmet come to your home?" I responded, "I told you I don't know anything. Surely my husbands' friends used to visit us but this cannot be a crime! We sometimes had gatherings with my friends."

They exaggerated everything so much that they even reviewed my son's cartoon videos and confiscated them. I got mad and eventually lost my temper. I shouted at a policeman, "Stop this nonsense! Isn't it clear that these are only cartoons? How could you take them as criminal evidence?" In a very angry manner he said, "How can I know its content?" I asked him how he could confiscate something as criminal evidence without knowing its content but he could not give any answer.

Finally, after searching my home for hours, they confiscated my kids' and sister in law's computers, my cell phones and many other things. I reacted since it was my work phone. There were private pictures of my clients that I was using in my social media accounts after I received permission. All the phone numbers of my clients and all my business life was in that cell phone. I begged them to take the others and to leave that one with me but they did not listen. As they were leaving with all our belongings, they did not give us any documentation. The meaning of this was that we would never be able to get back our laptops, tablets, cell phones which were holding all our memories of our past including my kids' baby pictures and videos.

To make matters worse, the police brought the building manager and the janitor with them. Many bad rumors were going to spread among my neighbors. We were one of the first families who were raided by the police after July 15th and both my husband's absence and the police raid to our home was going to result in much gossip and lies about us. Things were going to get so bad that I sometimes would not be able to enter the apartment building. I would go to my shop, work, and come back, and cry. This was all I could do. My world had been turned completely upside down.

The suffering spreads to my children

In addition to all this tragedy, my kids' school was shut down in the following days. As I mentioned previously, there was no better school in the city. God knows that I never worried for my kids when they were in that school. We were able to obtain all the education for science, social activities, and character. Both my husband and I were very busy at our jobs, so we could not pick up the kids from the school on time. But I always found the teachers caring my kids. I did not even worry about my kids for a single day while they were there.

This beautiful school was now shut down, like thousands of other schools in the country. Which school were we going to send our children to? Would they be able to adjust to the new school? Everything was up in the air and were all unknown.

Eventually, one of my family friends helped me enroll my kids in a neighborhood school with his children. Our goal was to keep the kids together and so that they could overcome these problems more easily. Unfortunately, while attending the school, the principal asked for a bribe shamelessly and insulted us as well. He said, "You used to give a lot of money to that private school, so you should give us money as well!" And unfortunately, the friend of ours had to bribe the principal to be able to have him enroll our kids. There was no justice left in the country and as a result there was no place we could file a complaint.

On the first day of school, in order for my kids to adapt more easily, I went to school with them. I was trying to keep them from any insults and did not leave them alone. Unfortunately, the government made a big propaganda video about the July 15th coup and at the beginning of school all parents and students had to watch it. They were spreading lies and claiming that Fethullah Gülen was an evil person, that he was Jewish and an enemy of Turks, and his sympathizers were all immoral people who were trying to take over the world. With all these lies, they were polarizing all the people in the country. There was a countrywide witch-hunt against the members of Hizmet and my kids hated the school the very first day. I consoled them and told them not to be sad. I told them their father was not a bad person and did not hurt anybody.

My son, who was in the middle school, was unfortunately going to be isolated by his teacher and classmates in the following days. He was well-educated in his previous school and could not adapt to his new school. His classmates were messing with him and as a result he got involved in some fights. I learned this later and he told me that he could not take it when they said bad things about his father.

Heaven becomes hell

In the following days, the social pressure increased so much that I could not even get in or out of my home. As a matter of fact, since my mother-in-law was taking care of my baby, I had begun to stay in her home. I heard that there were more police raids in my home and finally I decided to sell it.

This was naturally not easy for my kids and myself. I did not have my husband, friends, or school environment that we had before. Absolutely nothing! In addition to all of this, one of my clients took a picture of the "For Sale" sign in the window and shared it with everybody. I felt so humiliated. It would not be true if I said I never got depressed but for a while, I didn't even leave my home. As I was doing this, they would end up spreading more rumors that I had gone to jail.

We moved to my mother-in-law's home, but my father-in-law was a difficult person. My sister-in-law was attending university in Istanbul and my mother-in-law was staying with her during the school semester. However, since I gave birth and alongside this I was facing a lot of problems, she decided not to leave me alone and stayed with us. As a solution to not get her daughter in trouble, she sent my father-in-law instead and she stayed with me.

However, after a while, my father-in-law came back. Apparently, there was a problem between them. He began to complain to his wife about us. "We look after them. Let somebody else take care of them. You will come with me to Istanbul or else I will divorce you!" Before we could figure out what was happening, they immediately went to Istanbul for a few days. This would make our lives even more difficult because my baby had gotten used to her grandmother and I had to find someone to look after her.

I couldn't find anyone that was willing to babysit. I even offered to pay beforehand if someone would accept. Nobody did. I asked my sister and she accepted. Something was wrong with my baby, we were not able to calm her down. She cried so much that we decided to take her to the doctor. The doctor was going to tell me that the baby's ear was perforated and this was too much pain even for an adult. I began to ignore my job because I wasn't able to focus on it. I was busy with my baby's recovery and was still trying to get her used to her aunt. By this time, we had sold our home and car and I was not going out often. Even though there were so many rumors going on about me, I was still thanking God for my situation. People were feeling sorry for me and nobody was reporting me to the police. I was very sure that I would go to jail if someone reported me. Many mothers were going to jail with their babies and these were such horrible days for everybody.

The end of semester break was over and my mother-in-law was back. I was going to leave the baby with them, go to work, and see all the people who were talking behind my back, speaking sarcastically while smiling at my face, and asking ridiculous questions. I was following my husband's advice and not responding or arguing with them. I only argued with a girl who had been one of my customers for years. She was well-educated and was usually very nice, and it hurt that these people, who were previously so kind and considerate, began treating me with so much disgust and animosity. One day she said, "Sister, I want to ask you a question if you don't mind. They claim that you are a courier and that you transfer money in suitcases when you go abroad. Is that true?"

It was such a stupid question that caused me to finally lose my cool and snap. I said, "Don't take it wrong, but if I were so rich why would I work as a hairdresser and put up with the bad breath of people like you? I would stay home and take care of three kids happily. Besides, do I fly on a private jet so I can carry money in suitcases? I fly in the economy class and the amount of money I can carry is already limited. Please add some intelligence to your question!"

There was certainly a decline in the number of my customers over time. Some people stopped coming to my shop, while others who were telling me that they liked me but not my ideas. The ones who were still my customers were the ones who really liked my business or the ones who wanted to gossip. Sometimes they were trying to talk behind my back with my employees and get information about me by asking questions. God knows that I never responded to them and ignored them.

I was not surprised by the rumors that spread about us or by the people who were happy with the police raids to my home. I was only feeling pity for them. Our family was very established in this town, and even my mother who passed away 18 years ago was born here. I mean, these people knew us from our babyhood and they also appreciated my husband a lot. My husband always looked after my sisters, provided education for them, and helped them get married. Now, all of a sudden, he happened to be a terrorist! It saddened me greatly that most of the people that we grew up with and knew for so long turned on us so quickly.

By now, it had been about a year since my husband went to America. He had to apply for asylum since his passport had expired. We were living among the people who lost their mind in this open air prison. Our passports were canceled and he had to stay abroad due to the fear of arrest. We had to accept our destiny and were waiting for the day when our Lord would make us come together again.

During this time because of the problems I was having with my father-in-law, I had to rent a home in my sister's name and buy a small car. I found a good school and enrolled my kids there. Although my husband was not there, we managed to somewhat get our lives together. However, we were still living in a state of fear and uncertainty.

Things only continued to get much worse because the government constantly increased their brutality and illegality under the State of Emergency. We began to hear that they were arresting women whose husbands fled the country and that they were also giving the kids of those families to orphanages. Their goal was to force their main target to come back to Turkey. As the number of these cases began to increase, my husband and I became really anxious with the fear of facing the same problems. Every day was yet another uncertainty, as we never knew what the government might decree or if they would separate us against our will.

My husband and I would talk on the phone every day. We would constantly cry and could not even imagine how we would cope if our family was so forcibly separated. We never knew if that day's phone call would be our last one with each other. I was trying to hide my agony from my kids but whenever I happened to see a policeman, I either changed my way, hid, or if I was in the car lowered my head down. Our life was based on fear and we were continuously in a state of anxiety.

Enough is enough

Our situation had become so unbearable that we realized we had to leave Turkey. However, we could not just fly out because our passports were no longer valid. I had no idea how to go about the process of escaping without "normal" ways, but my husband told me to leave it to him. I got excited and regained my hope.

One day he called me whispering and told me to find $50,000, go to a certain park, and give the money to a guy that would be waiting there. I was confused, but still I asked a friend to do it for me. After a while, that friend called me in panic and told me that someone took the money and left! The guy told him that he was going to bring the passports but there was no way to be sure. We did not know this person, where he lived, or did not even have a way to contact him. There was nothing to do and I could only say "I trust God and there is nothing to do but wait."

Finally, after a nervous couple of weeks of waiting, my husband called me again. I only figured out when he began to say mysterious words like, "Same place...Go there again..." It was like a movie scene and I went there and began to wait. What was the guy like? How would I know him? I did not know anything. Eventually, I saw a hand stretching from behind me and dropping a plastic bag next to me. In that shocking moment, I didn't even dare to look around, took the bag, and saw our passports inside. My husband reminded me many times not to leave the passports at home. In the following days, I was going to keep the passports with me at all times. We spent a huge amount of money on them and I was literally stuck to them until I received a phone call from my husband.

He called me again and told me that we had to go to a harbor city. A relative of mine was going to meet with us there. I was going to tell my kids that we were going on a vacation but that they could take only one pair of shoes and clothes with them. They were confused about what kind of vacation it was. I told them we were going to buy more when we arrived there and their father arranged this vacation. They did not question further when I stated this, and even cheered up a bit.

I was going to be even more shocked when I arrived. We stayed in my relative's home and my husband called me and told me that we were going to go to Greece by boat. I was absolutely shocked because I thought we were going to take a flight. I began to cry. I could never ever do this! I could not dare do this! My relative said, "Sister don't get me wrong but not with three kids, even if I were only by myself, I would still not take this risk." And this made me even more scared. My husband got mad and told our relatives not to scare me. He told them not to interfere and asked me to make up my mind because he wanted the best for his family.

I requested some time to think over it and hung up the phone. My relative was still saying the same. I knew my husband was a person with common sense. This was something I tested so many times in my 18-year marriage. Whenever I did not listen to him, I always regretted it and suffered. He never misled me in the past. Finally, I made up my mind and decided to go as he said.

We had to go to another city. I was feeling as if I was going to my death. I later learned that our relatives cried a lot for us. At the end, we started a journey which we did not know whether it was going to be a reunion with or separation from our loved ones.

We spent a huge amount of money but it was apparently a very well-organized trip. One cab driver was taking us and after a while transferring us to another cab. After a nervous stay for 10 days in this harbor city, without knowing what was waiting for us, we started our journey on boat.

Escape from hell

On the 22nd of August we boarded a luxurious boat that resembled a cruise yacht. We were told that our trip would take approximately 9 hours. The captain was going to take us to our destination by visiting different places. What was waiting for us was not only uncertainty and fear, but also seasickness! We were terribly dizzy and were throwing up continuously. It was so bad that even though there was nothing left in our stomach, we were still vomiting. I began to think that we could not complete that trip. I called my husband and had to tell him our situation and apologized to him for not continuing our trip.

In a state of panic, he was going to contact the middleman and hear the answer that we were okay and vomiting was not a big problem when you compare it to staying back. It was maybe easy for him but neither me nor my kids had any strength to go on. My husband called me again and begged me to endure some more and told me that everything would be better with God's help. All in all, he was trying to ensure that we would reach him safely and quickly.

My kids and I decided to be patient no matter what happened to us. I am grateful to the captain because he sped up a bit and we arrived at a Greek island in several hours. It was an awkward feeling and we were one step closer to being a family again.

The person who met with us helped us move to a home where we were going to stay for 4 days. He provided us with our needs, purchased our flight tickets, and took us to an airport. He said "You will continue alone from this point." Our tickets were for Brussels and our friends from the Hizmet Movement were going to meet us there.

In a state of nervousness, we began to wait for the check-in process. The passports were real but because we left Turkey illegally, there was no seal on them. They immediately took us to a police station. We were terrified that we would be sent back to Turkey! Loneliness, despair, being like a refugee in a foreign country in a police station with my three kids, the language barrier... My older son was trying to communicate with his limited English and my baby was crying continuously. Helplessly, I called my husband and told him that we were detained. He requested to talk with the police. In fact, this was not possible under normal circumstances but since he felt sad for my helplessness and fear, the police commander accepted this request.

My husband had a long talk with the man and told him that we were not criminals, and were instead fleeing from a dictator's brutality. He begged the police commander to let us leave and continue onwards. The police commander checked his watch and told me that we should hurry because our plane was about to take off. I cannot express how much we were relieved. I was thankful since we could overcome this obstacle. We took the plane without facing any problems and flew to Brussels comfortably.

Hello Europe!

A young couple who were members of the Hizmet Movement met us in Brussels. It was so cold for us after Turkey and the island that they took off their jackets and put them on my kids. In order to make us feel more comfortable, they offered to take us to a hotel which they had already reserved. But we were so scared and anxious that we were shaking. I told them honestly that me and my kids were so afraid, we did not want to go to a hotel and would like to stay at their home with them. The young wife was a lovely person. She smiled warmly and stated that it would be an honor for them to host us in their home.

That woman, whom I did not know at all, hosted us so nicely that it was impossible not to be impressed. Her husband was going to stay at his mother's home to make us feel more comfortable and we were going to take a good sleep in a peaceful place after all these difficulties we had. We happened to find ourselves at a wonderful breakfast in the morning.

Later that day, we shopped for winter clothes for my kids and myself. After staying there for a few days, we went to Germany with the help of the beautiful people of Hizmet one of whom even gave the keys to his home to us, to people whom they did not know, so we could stay while he was away.

My husband told me that we would stay in Germany for 15 days but the length of time increased to one month. The Eid holiday was just ahead. We were going to spend our time there but would not be bored for even a single day. Each day we were guests to new hosts who showed us around, and served food to us. Indeed, none of those people were expecting anything in return and did it solely for the sake of God.

I had a chance to listen to their stories when I stayed in Germany. Some fascist Turks, who were supportive of the dictator in Turkey, unfortunately existed in Germany as well and were doing their best to give people like us a hard time. They started a social lynching campaign against Hizmet people, they were isolating them, attacking their shops, and spreading lies about them. Evil was evil everywhere. The victims of the dictator were unfortunately dealing with this kind of problems as well.

We say goodbye "three" times…

We were just getting used to Germany when my husband called and told us that we were going to fly to Mexico City. We said goodbye to everyone and went to the airport, only to realize we were one day early; we could not figure out the right time because of the time zone difference. We had to go back confused.

Same stress the next day...We packed up, said goodbye, and hit the road again. We were about to get in the airplane when my husband called and told me not to fly. He learned that a Turkish family was detained in Mexico and they were interrogated for hours. At first, this did not make any sense to me; what did this have to do with us? I was still thinking we were having a normal trip there; I later learned that it was the only point of entry where we could reunite with him. In order not to scare me more, he did not mention it.

But our luggage was already checked in. There was nothing to do. The luggage, plane tickets, hotel reservations had all been thrown away. We had to stay in Germany and we were confused. Our hosts were surprised to see us again at their doorstep, but they were extremely happy to have us back, for we got so connected with them.

We bought tickets for the following week and hit the road again. My older son said "Mom, please let's not say goodbye to each other this time, for God's sake! It is so weird if we have to come back again." Fortunately, we were going to make it this time. However, we were scared of leaving the airport since we did not have departure stamps on the passports. They were brand new and clean. My husband had warned me about being ready for all possibilities. Our situation was pretty much in the hands of the officer at the airport. We were either going to pass easily or wait for hours. I was doing what my husband told me to do. He told me to use body language to communicate with the officer and the kids not to speak at all.

When the officer asked me why there were no departure stamps in our passports, I was not going to say anything but made gestures to mean I did not know. The officer got mad and told me loudly to speak in English or German with him, but I would still remain silent. I continued this psychological battle for 15 minutes but would be able to pass eventually.

I could not believe that we made it as we sat in the plane. We had been really afraid. We were flying to Cancún and my husband relieved me by saying that two lawyers were waiting for us there. If we faced any challenges, they were going to help us.

Thankfully, we safely arrived in Cancún and passed through with no trouble. Some people met us there. As they were dropping us off at the hotel, they told us that we were going to stay there for 3 days. "For the sake of God, please take us in the shortest possible time! We do not want to wait anymore!" I said in a rather worn-out mood. As a response they said "We can take you but you will have jet-lag and cannot endure it." I begged him that I did not care and wanted to move on immediately, as early as in the morning if possible.

We moved to Mexico City by car early in the morning. After staying there for one night we took a flight to a border city. We were with our guide. On board, we were the only ones with a different skin color. The guide told us to pray so as not to be suspected and eventually be detained. We were very close to freedom.

We got out of the plane with prayers. We were faking to be happily chatting with my kids while I was having so much fear inside me which only God could know how much. However, I was also feeling that an invisible hand was going to take and help us! It was as if our fate was being written while we were walking alongside a narrow hallway. Eventually, a soldier touched my shoulder and I felt an extreme amount of fear suddenly wash over me. Luckily, it was only to warn me to put our luggage on the X-Ray device.

Finally, we were going to leave the airport. The guide told me that his part was finished then and we were going to continue by ourselves. He was going to take us to the border and we were going to walk from that point. To make matters worse, we were not going to have our phones anymore either. For the last time, I talked with my husband and the lawyer in Mexico. The lawyer told us that we needed to pass the border and that he would follow us and this trip would be difficult but that we did not need to worry. We were starting another stressful trip again!

The Mexican border

Our guide left us at the Mexican border after having us eat food. He wished us luck and we began to walk quickly with our luggage in our hands. We were amidst a sea of refugees, who all looked like us and were probably feeling a similar fear of sorts inside. We were speeding up as those around us sped up, causing everyone else to speed up even more. There was a shared feeling of desperation amongst the group, and we all knew it.

Out of breath, we finally reached the end of the long line. As I gave our passports to the officer, I forgot what I was going to say. Our lawyer made me repeat it many times, but the word "asylum" did not come to my mind. I began to panic. Eventually, my son typed the sentence "We seek asylum" into our cellphone and showed it to the border agents.

They then took us to another room. When they wanted us to take off our earrings, necklaces, and belts, we thought we were granted asylum and were very happy. We foolishly thought we were being welcomed in and then would be allowed to move on easily. Within the next few hours we were going to be able to figure out that this would not be the case and that our stress would continue. Eventually, they took us through an endless, freezing cold hallway. Every door was locked behind us, and we quickly felt our warmth and certainty fade away. We marched onward but our anxiety rose with every minute that passed. Eventually, they told me one of the things that I had feared most throughout this entire trip: that my older son could not accompany me anymore. I did not understand why and began to get hysterical.

They separated us while we were in tears. I was crying while my son was screaming "Mom!" The little ones also began to burst into tears too but they forced us to separate. They were going to take us to the dorm for women and children and my older one was going to be taken to the dorm for adult men. I could not speak English and as if that is not bad enough, now they were separating me from my son. Our cries were echoing throughout the hallways. We had serious trauma and left each other in tears. My poor son cried so much and kicked the walls that they decided to let us see each other for 10 minutes after which we were separated again. We were both scared, helpless, and did not know what was waiting for us.

We were put in a very cold room. The room had no windows or clock, and we did not know how long we had been there or whether it was day or night. I wrapped my little ones around and I was just about to fall asleep when the big iron door cracked open noisily. One man came in and announced my name.

They took me to interrogation, and fortunately I could express myself with the help of a certified online interpreter. They asked me all kinds of questions such as, "Why did you pass the border? Who, and what, are you? What was your previous job, and where were you born?" I told them that my family and my husband's family were members of the Hizmet Movement and I was a sympathizer as well. I told them that I was seeking asylum since we did not have safety in Turkey and they could take my kids away from me there. I had a lot of trouble but I could not live without my kids. As they listened to me the officer began to understand our situation, apologized for treating us badly, and stated that they did not know what happened to us. Afterwards, they were going to be incredibly nice to me and my son who was staying in another room. Even, one of the policemen visited my son and consoled him that it was a temporary process and it had to be like that for a while.

I would end up separated from my son despite their kindness, which caused me to cry quite often. Then, I was going to be interrogated under oath. All in all, what I was telling them was not fiction: I told them our story over and over because it was the truth. We were law abiding citizens that paid taxes and did not commit crimes, and that the government staged a fake coup in order to name hundreds of thousands of innocent people as terrorists. Finally, they asked me what I expect from the US. I said "Nothing. I only want my most basic human right: to be free."

We were going to stay there for the following 2 days. To know that my poor son's eyes were getting bloodshot and not having an appetite to eat anything was pushing my patience. Even though it was only two days it felt like twenty days. I was crying here and he was crying there. At last, I wanted them to let my other son stay with his elder brother by using hand signs. They fortunately did not deny my request because my older one was going to tell me later "Everybody was speaking Spanish around, the lights were too bright, the mattresses were on the floor, the toilets were getting plugged, I could not sleep at all and was about to go insane. As he came, I began to talk and was relieved with his help."

In my case, I was getting my courage from my baby. In the days that felt like centuries to us, even though he could not speak, I was talking to him in a language that only mothers know, holding his hand while he was sleeping and gaining strength from him. I surrounded him with blankets and when I made a signal that he was sleeping, nobody was approaching us.

Then, they transferred us to another place by bus. In our new place, we were staying in a police station like place during the day time and then being taken to a place that resembled a hotel at night. We were not allowed to keep our doors closed but at least we had private restrooms and beds. My baby could unfortunately not take any other food but mother milk. He was naturally not able to eat the sandwiches given to us. We were receiving one cup of milk and were grateful even for this. The same routines were in place every day. We were searched every time we would get on the buses to the hotel rooms and were taken to different rooms all the times. It was the same for days and nights.

We got our hopes up too early again on the 10th day, when they said they were going to release us. The kids were so happy that they were eventually going to see their father. We were grouped into 3 families each and each group had two officers.

One of the officers told my son that we looked like rich people and how come he was not traveling in New York like his peers but ended up here. My awesome son responded to him in a mature way and said "This is how it was meant to be."

We were going to have our biggest embarrassment yet as we were taken to the airport. They first took us to a room similar to a laundromat and made us wear tracksuits after taking off all of our clothes, including the baby's. All of the groups were dressed the same color. These tracksuits made us stand out in the crowd and labeled us as fugitives. I was so embarrassed and sad that I could not keep my head up and look at anybody's face.

Later on, I was going to learn that one officer asked my son why I was so sad, to which my son said that I was very careful with I wore and that I was not happy with the tracksuits. The officer felt sorry for that they gave back my shoes and jacket, and the kids' sweaters. I was at least able to get rid of the slippers on my feet and this relieved me a little.

I was planning to meet my husband when I got off of the airplane and was relieved with the thought of this nightmare finally ending. As the plane landed, I requested the officers to give me my pants back since I did not want my husband to see us in these tracksuits. Unfortunately, the female officer told me that I needed to be a little more patient and that I still needed to keep the tracksuits on.

Yet another camp!

Our plane landed and we got into a car to be taken to yet another unknown location. It was raining extremely heavily and we were going to have another trip full of fear through muddy fields. We finally arrived and saw a group of trailers that were placed in the middle of a scary field that was fenced with barbed-wire similar to that of a prison. We continued to wear our tracksuits, got our X-Rays taken, and gave blood tests all over again. They also asked more questions such as, "Have you been raped or harassed sexually? Are you pregnant?" In hindsight these were completely normal questions to ask, however in that moment I felt humiliated and began to cry. Luckily we have never had those kinds of problems but it had apparently occurred with other fugitives. It was like this nightmare would never end!

Afterwards, we went to have our photos taken. My nerves were shot and I was crying continuously. I felt like I was trapped in a perpetual hell of instability, separation, and fear. My eyes were bloodshot when they took my photo. They already contacted my husband and I was going to cry more as I heard his voice.

We arrived that day at 6 am, and at midnight we finally got to go to sleep in one of those trailers. We were explicitly told not to close the curtains or never to go outside at all. We were extremely tired and fell asleep almost immediately. We were sleeping for almost an hour until we were awoken and taken out again. I mustered whatever strength I had and took the baby and left but I felt like I was nearing the end of my rope.

In the office that we were taken there were a lot of papers for us to sign. We were dumbfounded as the officers left after we signed the papers. What were we waiting for? All of a sudden, and completely out of the blue, my husband came inside! That moment was indescribable. It was as if we had not seem him in an eternity. All of us hugged him and we began to cry. We hugged each other, cried, cried, and cried…

In the following 17 days, we were going to stay in that camp and my husband was going to visit us from time to time. Despite him being there, I cannot define how difficult it was. We were going to different places every day. For example, we would wait for the kid's shots and as we were waiting in line they became sick and then would have to go to the doctor's line, and then the medicine line. They also only gave enough medicine for minimum usage. People were blowing their noses on their clothes and there were flies all over the place. A healthy person would get sick in that doctor line!

Food was another problem, because they mostly cooked Mexican food that we could not eat because it was not halal (permissible for Muslims to consume). My children could barely eat anything. But they never treated us badly. The cafeteria workers were very loving and kind, and showed us so much warmth. The woman who was distributing the food was giving extra pot soup and pointing at the baby to make me feed him. They were so happy for us the day we were finally leaving the camp.

Days were passing and we were somehow getting used to the camp. One day, they suddenly called in a group of us for an interview. As I was waiting my turn, my name was going be announced. It was pronounced correctly for the first time in this entire journey to my absolute surprise. There was a young officer whose father was Turkish and mother German who apologized to me for not being aware of us after such a long stay. She really felt sad for us that we had to stay there with a little baby. I was thanking her over and over again but she was telling me that it was her responsibility to help us. Indeed, my kids and I were suffering from vomiting and diarrhea, and the baby was not able to make his toilet since he was not eating much. We were also not allowed to bring food from outside. In short, we were all miserable.

Our nightmare ends

Finally, the day that we had dreamed of for many months had finally dawned. We were at the end of the gathering adventure, which took weeks. The camp workers came and hugged us and said goodbye to us as if they were our family. As we were leaving with my husband and kids I said "Alhamdulillah! Alhamdulillah! (Thank you God!)

It has not been a very long time since we have started a new life. We are hoping that the bad days we had are gone forever. We basically had to reset our lives and start from scratch in a land that is unfamiliar to us. We also feel sad deep down because we were fortunate enough to have escaped Turkey while so many other innocent people are still arrested, trapped in that hell. We feel sad, cry, and pray to God for them, but we have to hold on to life as well.

My husband was a hardworking person in Turkey. He used to help everybody. He sometimes went too far to the point of neglecting us while he was helping other people in need. To be honest, our family ties got stronger recently. We lean on each other more because we felt the absolute agony of being separated.

Contrary to many friends of ours, we have been able to bring our savings from our asset's sales. This made starting over much easier for us. Even though I cannot perform my job here, my husband started a new business. Our Lord gave us a chance for a new start and hopefully our other friends will be able to do the same.

3

Exile

A.K.

Alienation

I was once regarded as a well-respected and admired academician in Turkey. That changed overnight. Everyone around me started to disappear. Those who used to smile at me started to look the other way. Those who praised my character, career, and diligence started to talk behind my back. I was declared an "enemy of the state." They had already chosen their side and I was left on the opposite side. It seems that I had chosen my fate when I had decided to speak out against my government whose corrupt leaders were exposed in a huge police investigation in December 2013. I had aligned myself with those who bravely shouted "The emperor has no clothes."

I was an academic who had built a career in political science at one of Turkey's most prominent universities. I would describe how people treated me as "ignorance," but ignorance can be cured. What I endured was not something that can be rectified by education. The "ignorance" I saw was without any remedy.

First, the articles that I submitted to the university's journal were not being published even though they had already passed the peer-review process. My international conference trips were being investigated. Although approved by the administration, my travel expenses were not being reimbursed. I was facing an intensive campaign of mobbing and passive aggression. The university did not want me to speak out against the government. They expected me to act like an ostrich and simply stick my head in the sand to ignore any injustices that were occurring.

I could have kept my silence as a person or a regular citizen, but how was I supposed to remain silent as a political scientist? How could I maintain my self-respect if I hid the truth while speaking about Turkish foreign policy in conferences? This was impossible for me to do.

The day everything changed

It is well-known in political science that dictators will often produce sources of legitimacy in order to purge opposing groups. The coup attempt on July 15, 2016 was planned to legitimize the purge, right from the very first few minutes. Three to five hundred people hit the streets in a few cities, and it was very obvious that this was a plot.

My wife and I were visiting her grandmother in Istanbul on the night of the coup attempt and were catching up over a cup of tea. We were all happy since my brother, who was a police officer in a different city at the time, was also with us during his annual holiday break. After seeing the "coup attempt" rumor on Twitter, we turned on the TV. Although Turkey has a history of coups, I was too young to witness a coup in person but knew a lot about Turkey's previous coups because of the extensive research that I had done on them in the past. From what I had known, curfew was soon to be declared, so we went back home.

The hours following the coup were very strange and abnormal. The government was quick to point out the Hizmet Movement as the perpetrators of the coup even though we were already being oppressed by the government for several years. We were seriously concerned this time because it was obvious that the government would blame the coup on us and make us suffer. My wife, mother, father, brother, and I all couldn't fall asleep and watched the news all night.

By morning we were all exhausted and were getting ready to go to sleep when my brother, Ali, a decorated police officer, received a phone call. He was being called back on duty. We were scared, and rightfully so. Ali was exiled to provincial areas of the country once the government's oppression of Hizmet affiliated people had begun years ago. His work situation continued to deteriorate as he faced intensive bullying from his superiors, and his place was being changed every twenty days. They even threatened to kill his kids. My brother promptly left home to go to wherever he was summoned to. We did not know it at the time, but that would be the last time we would see him as a healthy person.

My brother, who was already on antidepressants for a while, was going to get sick within a week and would get transferred to a mental hospital. His illness got worse because of the high dose of medication he received during his 35-day treatment there. And while he was still in the hospital, on a Saturday, he was going to get arrested by his former colleagues.

My dad accompanied Ali during his 35-day hospital stay and had begged the doctors to release him because he was losing his mind day by day from all of the medication that he was on. However, like most other people in the country, the doctors were inhumane. Ali had already become addicted to the medication when one day they took him to an undisclosed place. We wouldn't hear from him for a while.

I received a call from the university where I used to work and was told that the police were coming for me and that I had to go to give a statement. I did so without any hesitation because I did not have anything to hide. The police did indeed come, search my home thoroughly, and then wrote a report and left since they couldn't find anything. Afterwards, I was discharged by the board of the university. I pleaded to be reinstated but was denied. I then left for the city where my brother was staying. Before I reached my destination, my neighbors called me and told me that the police came back with a locksmith, broken into my home, and rifled through everything inside. They had already been there two days before and ended up not finding anything again.

I had travelled to my brother's city for his court hearing. My brother was finally able to appear in court after he was secretly questioned under torture. At the end of the hearing, my brother and around 100 former police officers who were facing the same charges, except those who had "confessed," were arrested and sent to prison. I was going to find him very miserable and broken, sobbing like a little child, when I visited him in prison a week later.

Getting arrested

A while later I went to visit my brother in prison. I was taken to a room where I thought I was going to meet my brother, but I was attacked by soldiers who were hiding in the room. They were all acting like they had caught a con artist or a serial killer who was on the run for a long time. They were very cruel to me. I was taken to the police station with two other people and made to wait there for hours. I found out that the other two people were both taken in for criminal activity. Not surprisingly, the prosecutor charged me while letting the other two go.

I had to go to court for the first time in my life. That was where I was going to find out about the indictment against me. A while ago, a friend from my former university had called me and made an offer. We had taken out a loan from a bank, Bank Asya, and purchased land and a house. During this process, I had sent my friend some money, and because of this I was charged with "transferring money in support of terrorism" (because the bank we transferred money through was affiliated with the Gülen – Hizmet – movement). That friend of mine was also arrested and tortured. Furthermore, we had bought an apartment from someone who had a completely different worldview from the Movement's who was also arrested. I explained to the judge that all the transactions were legal and reasonable. There is a Turkish saying that goes, "When the wolf is determined to eat the lamb, he would say he was punishing her for she was mudding the water while drinking from it." That was exactly what I was going through. They wouldn't believe or understand me. I eventually reached a point where I could not take it anymore and simply smiled at this sham court.

They took me out of the courtroom in handcuffs. My mother, father, and wife were all crying while I, on the other hand, was emotionally deadened. My only concern was my daughter who was not there. Who knows how long she was going to cry, or for how long she won't be able to see me at home? For the last few years, I had been watching her quietly and getting upset every morning before I would leave her, thinking that it would be the last time I would see her. Thankfully, the soldiers allowed me to take a video to send to her. I smiled at my wife's phone camera, hiding the handcuffs. I told my daughter, "I love you so much! I love you so much, but I have some things to do, and we will be apart for a while. I don't know for how long." I also took a few pictures full of smiles and kisses. We probably looked very tragicomic from the outside: A man in handcuffs giving kisses and smiling to a camera held by a crying woman. The last thing I saw, while I was being pushed into the police car, was my father and my wife hugging each other and sobbing.

The ward of death

The prison was a place where the living conditions were very tough and survival was not guaranteed. I saw people like Saban and Mustafa, who couldn't see the sunlight inside their 4–5 square meter (43–54 square feet) cells, a person named Ahmet, who was beaten until his cheekbone was broken and then thrown into his cell. On top of that, his wife was thrown into jail along with his 1.5-year-old son. I also saw inmates who were beaten, tortured, and even perished after melting away right in front of my eyes because of a lack of medical treatment.

It was 11:35 at night. Since I had high blood pressure, they took me to the patients' ward. All of the inmates, who were jailed because of similarly alleged crimes, woke up and came to me; a professor with heart failure; an old man with liver failure who used to work at the district governorship; another old man with a serious case of diabetes who was working as a driver at Zaman Newspaper; and more than anybody else, medical doctors. All of them were above the age of 60 and were very distinguished people. I stepped into the ward, which had a maximum capacity of 4 people, as the 13th inmate (and we would be 14 two days later), and was given a blanket after I told them my story. There were no beds, so I had to sleep on the floor.

It was a cold night. It was so cold in the winters that the windows and the doors of the ward would freeze with about 1 inch of ice on them. Although it was mid-September, it was an unbelievably cold night. On my first night, I laid the blanket on the floor and made a pillow out of some prayer rugs and shivered from the cold until the morning. I eventually did see the morning, but how I got through the night was like nothing else.

I had two apartments that I had purchased with my honest earnings. My wife told me once, "If they ever arrest you then I'll sell both apartments and get the best lawyer to save you." My answer was always "Relax, there won't be a need to do such a thing." However, my first night on that hard floor made me think twice, and I knew that I would give up those two apartments, for which I had worked for years, just to save myself from that place. It was a dreadful shock! Every day I was waking up to find myself in the same place! I was opening my eyes hoping that it would be a dream every single time.

I hoped that I would get used to it in the following days, but when I thought about it, which I had a lot of time to do, I only began to feel worse over time. The president of the university I used to work at was sentenced to 28 years of jail time despite his innocence. I had friends who were sentenced to four consecutive life sentences for no legitimate reason. Many of my friends faced terrible punishments. What was going on left no more endurance in me. What was going to happen now?

This uncertainty was testing my sanity. I did not even know what I was being accused of. I thought for days if I were to be sent to prison for a long time how old would my daughter be when I was out? I could stay in prison, but would it be possible that she did not grow up so that I wouldn't miss those beautiful, early days?

Even as grown-ups, we hadn't understood what was happening. How could we possibly explain this to a 4-year-old? I was able to see my daughter only once in the next two months. They allowed her to stay for only 20 minutes even though it was a two-hour visiting session. She cried, hugged, and begged me, "Dad, please, let's go home!" but the guards sent me back inside by force. Can you imagine the trauma that she went through?

Sunlight was a luxury

We used to wake up at 3:30 a.m. for the (voluntary) night prayers and then again at 5:00 a.m. for the morning prayers. I was a faithful person who believed in God and never missed my prayers but the recent upheaval in society caused me to question my faith. I was still practicing my religion and performing my prayers, but I couldn't help but think, "I was innocent, so why did God allow me to be in here?" My mind, and eventually my faith, were slowly unraveling right before my very eyes.

I was extremely sensitive about hygiene and noise and thus had a very hard time in the ward. One of the inmates gave me his bed in the morning because I couldn't sleep during the first night. There was barely a foot of space between my face and the ceiling, which was full of mold, and the whole room was only 30 square meters (about 323 square feet) and contained 13 people. It was like a cave. I was about to go insane!

We could go to the yard between 8:00 a.m. and 4 p.m. By "yard" I don't mean an outdoor area. It was essentially a relatively larger room that saw no sunlight and had an area of 50 square meters (about 538 square feet) and a height of 10 meters (about 33 feet). There were holes on the walls between adjacent yards through which you could speak to other inmates.

I was in the yard one day and was speaking to a voice from the other side of the wall. I did not know what he looked like; all I knew was that he was an inmate who had been sentenced to solitary confinement. The voice said that he had been here for 24 years for partaking in the Madimak Incidents of 1993, in which 33 people were killed during protests. I asked him when he would be released: "When I die," he replied, "I got a life sentence." He had 5 children with whom he did not have a chance to share anything beautiful with. He was a dead man to them. "I did not do anything," he said, the only "crime" that he committed was protesting.

In my previous life, just like the people living outside, I would have thought that he would not have been in prison if he wasn't guilty. However, I came to understand it then as I had experienced firsthand how the state machine grinds its victims. I hadn't done anything either, yet there I was. If a man who had not done anything had been in prison for 24 years then it was quite possible for me to share the same fate as him. And this fear caused me to tremble. I understood that there were worse fates for people other than death.

Begging for mercy

We resorted to reading books during most nights as it was usually too difficult to sleep. There were cells for solitary confinement on top of the wards and the groaning inmates could often
be heard above us. Every night we would hear one of them
screaming between the bars, "I cannot take it anymore, God,
please take away my life!" every single night. Their suffering
had become so unbearable that the idea of death and its mer-
ciful release started to not sound so bad. His friends had been
dying over the years and he was going to die too before he got
to laugh, eat his favorite meal, love and be loved. There were
people among the prisoners who had been sentenced to 150
years. The ones who would be out in 2035 or even 2050. That
was, of course, if they survived that long. There was a 28-year-
old young man who used to give us haircuts; he was sentenced
to 55 years. What if I ended up like that? Everyone in the ward
was using antidepressants because it was unbearable otherwise. This was a prison where hopes and dreams were merci-
lessly destroyed.

It was an extremely overcrowded cell. There was no bed for
me to sleep on; so I was sleeping on a one-inch mattress on the
floor in that cold weather. I put newspapers, books, and what-
not underneath it to keep the cold away. The skin of my hands
would dry and crack because I had to hand-wash my laundry.
I would hide my hands to keep them away from my mother's
eyes when she visited me. At night people used to step on me
to go to the toilet and sewage would drip on me from the cells
above.

There was only one restroom for all of us, and there was
hot water for only half an hour per day. While we were try-

ing to figure out how to share this hot water, water shortages, each lasting up 5–6 hours, started happening at least three days a week. Of course, it was all intentional to make things even harder on us. They were even cutting the strings that we dried our clothes on.

The people they pestered were mostly sick and elderly. There was a former employee of a district governorship with a severe liver disease (Hepatitis B). The man needed urgent medical attention, but they only released him just before he died.

Another prisoner was a well-known professor who had leg surgery. Think about it – the man had screws and stitches in his leg! They sent him back to the ward from the hospital only after one and a half days with cuffs in his legs! He needed to have stayed at the hospital for at least a month. He was an old man who couldn't do anything for himself, even go to the restroom. For months, other inmates took turns cleaning his bed. I personally witnessed when the poor man prayed to God and asked for his death. His leg was getting thinner day by day and eventually developed an abscess which caused it to become permanently disabled.

It becomes hard for one to feel sad for themselves while witnessing such life changing and traumatizing tragedies. In fact, you forget about yourself sometimes and feel sad for the others even more because you are not alone, because there are people who are in worse conditions than you.

We had a former police officer whose story gained media coverage. He was very young, healthy, and was a very bright police officer. Because of the so-called coup attempt, he was sent to the same prison with us. He was tortured physically (his cheekbone was broken with an ashtray) and emotionally (his wife was arrested along with their baby). The poor guy became sick because of the torture and psychological pressure, and all of his petitions for release were swept under the mat. He was in perfect health when he was first put in prison and was eventually released from it while unconscious. He passed away a short time later.

These unbelievable events that we have seen, heard, and gone through first hand were a tragedy that you would only see in movies or novels.

A brotherly reunion

Winter had arrived, and it was very cold. The door of the ward was frozen with about 2 inches of ice on the inside and we were huddling together to not freeze in that 215 square feet space. It was like there was literally nothing good in our lives. Until, one day, my brother was sent to our ward at 2 o'clock.

It was so nice to see him, even in this place. We cried and hugged each other for a long time. He was going to make me cry even more in the coming days. He was given a lot of medication and had thus put on a lot of weight. Since there was no space to sleep, I started sharing my floor mattress with him. His closest friend and spiritual mentor had testified against him. Ali couldn't take what he was going through anymore and became depressed. He was just like a child; his hands and feet would shake uncontrollably; he would wake up in the middle of the night screaming for his mother and would hug me. Although seeing him like that was devastating for me, it made me forget about my own problems and thus allowed me to focus on making him feel better.

My brother did his best to help the other prisoners, and

myself, starting from the very moment he arrived to my ward. Since he knew a good deal about the petitioning process, he wrote petitions of objection for unjust imprisonment on behalf of everybody, one by one. Even for my imprisonment, he sent petitions of objection several times. And the decision for the continuation of my detention was overruled with the help of one of the petitions that he wrote. I was released on a cold February day!

Freedom...

I was not ecstatic when I was released from prison. I felt guilty that I was fortunate enough to leave while my brother, and the other inmates whom I had grown to consider my brothers, remained in that cold hell. I can say that it was the most miserable day of my life. They released me one evening after sunset. I floundered in knee-high snow, cried, and got on a bus to go to the city center. I knocked on the door of my home, not with excitement, but with shame. I was carrying the guilt of leaving my brother behind. And my mother's first question was, "Where is your brother?" I bowed my head and could not bring myself to answer.

I thought things would be better outside, but it was nothing like that. My daughter had become depressed after I was arrested. She began collecting pebbles from the street, and when asked the reason, she would reply "so that they wouldn't get lost."

My wife was five months pregnant at the time I went to prison, and she had a miscarriage because of the stress she went through. I felt like nothing would ever be the same. No one was talking to me anymore, except for a few friends, who called but couldn't speak because of crying and then hung up. I went to my old university to pick up my belongings but the dean did not even let me in. I was stubborn and resisted, and did not leave until I was finally able to get my personal belongings. However, not surprisingly, I was going to find out that they filed a complaint about this later on.

The fear

It was one and a half months after my release. My lawyer told me that there was another arrest warrant for me. The really difficult days were yet to start. The government imposed a restraining order over all of my properties. My close friends and relatives wouldn't see me. It was as if I had become some kind of high profile terrorist that was being hunted, and simultaneously ignored, by the entire country. I did not have any place to stay because the police would always raid the apartments of my mother and mother-in-law. I was hiding in the apartment of my wife's grandmother, living a fugitive life. I managed to tolerate this situation for 15 days.

I eventually gave up and realized that I couldn't stay in this country anymore. My passport had already been canceled a while ago, and as a last resort, I decided to leave the country. I did not know how to go about leaving, and the prospect of leaving seemed impossible considering every single escape route was flooded with police officers. Finally, a friend of mine, who was a lawyer, managed to arrange a meeting with some smugglers to take me out. We hit the road to Aksaray to meet with up with them. My wife and daughter were with me. When I kissed my daughter goodbye for the last time it was almost like she was aware of everything that was happening and was crying continuously. My poor daughter had become acquainted with that pain at the age of four.

The smugglers made me get into a car in the evening. There were three other people inside. None of us knew each other at all and nobody said a word. But our facial expressions said it all. Tension was extremely high. There was a police checkpoint in the entrance to Edirne, and they had stopped the car right behind us. We had dodged a bullet there.

We arrived at a border village. The Maritsa (Evros) River was visible just ahead. The smugglers left us right after sunset and ran away. We were left alone with our backpacks. Supposedly, someone would pick us up but no one showed. The smugglers had run away leaving a large bag behind, which apparently had an inflatable boat in it. It was too heavy to take with us, and thus we decided to leave it behind and move on.

Robbed and reported by locals

Four people that did not know each other and could not say a word to each other but unavoidably shared the same fate. While we were walking with our backpacks, we were suddenly surrounded by villagers. They were asking questions one after the other: "Who are you? What are you doing here? Where are you from? Where are you going?"

The smugglers had warned us firmly, "If you encounter anybody, do not speak in Turkish. Act like you are from Syria, otherwise they will report you to the police to receive bounty rewards!" We did not say a word and tried to express ourselves through body language in order to try and convince them to let us through, but they were not humane. They attacked us with sickles and looted our backpacks. They also seized our money and called the police. At that point, one of us ran away. I summoned my courage and started running after him.

I ran, and ran, and ran, and ran, and ran. It did not matter in what direction. I was just running into the darkness. I waded through swamps, tripped over rocks, and scraped my knees multiple times. Nevertheless, I did not stop. I don't remember for how long I ran without taking a break. Finally, I remember tumbling down in a wheat field after I couldn't manage to take another step. I laid down and watched the sky for 30 minutes. I had no idea what to do at this point. Before long I heard a military police unit passing not far.

Apparently, they were looking for me. While they were searching for me in the field I felt like I aged ten years in that short span of time as questions were rushing into my brain: "Do they have a thermal camera? Do they have their search dogs? If yes, I will be caught right away!" Thankfully, I did not get caught.

That gave me hope because it meant that I still had a chance to run away. But I was soaked to the skin, my shoes were full of water, and I was freezing! I had a mobile phone with me, and I inserted a sim card while my hands were shaking. I called the only number I memorized, my father's, by covering the phone to hide the lights it was emitting. I had not told my parents about my journey because they were old, and I did not want them to worry about me. I just asked my father to call my wife and tell her to call that number. When my wife called me, I asked her to call the middleman and let him know about my situation. During those phone conversations, I ran out of credit!

Minutes passed, and nobody called me. Maybe I did not have service, I did not know. After a while, I decided to stand up and walk towards the river. I started to hear dogs barking as I got close to the river which made me freak out. Just at that moment, the middleman called and told me, "We will pick you up, tell me your location." I was overjoyed, but as time passed, nobody came and I was facing the risk of freezing. Eventually, they called again just to tell me that I was on my own. I begged them and cried out, "I will die here if you don't show up, please help!" Of course, they did not show mercy. I wasn't worth anything to them.

Finally, a friend of mine and my father-in-law rented a car and headed towards me. I tried to move forward by crawling and tried to warm myself up by tucking pieces of grass inside my pants. I felt I was going to be waiting for a long time, God knows how long, and had to do my best not to freeze. I received a call again from them at around 5:00 am. They were about to arrive, and I passed through a forest full of thorns to reach the meeting point. My whole body was splintered and every part of me would be pricked, but I didn't care because I wanted to survive!

We finally managed to meet up around 7:30 a.m. I was all covered in mud and thorns. When I returned home, they would remove thorns from my body for an entire week, and more importantly, I would lay sick in bed like a corpse for three months. I wasn't getting better, but I couldn't go to the hospital either. I wished to die so many times!

Stuck in a hole

We started staying at my wife's grandparents. But they started to feel uncomfortable about our presence because they feared getting arrested. Our properties were confiscated, our credit cards were canceled, and my father had run out of money because of our legal and living expenses.

A friend of mine, who was a doctor and knew about our situation, risked it all and rented an apartment for me in one of those huge buildings where nobody knew each other. He furnished the apartment, took care of the utilities, gave us some money, and left.

My daughter was getting bored because of staying indoors all the time. I was not even able to take her to the park. I lived a prison life all day long in that apartment for seven months. We would turn the lights off at night in order to not draw attention to our apartment and would even put napkins in the peep-hole of the door. We were detached from the rest of the world and would read books all day long and follow the news on Twitter. Since I had a lot of free time, I was checking every statistic about how many smugglers were getting arrested and where.

After seven months, I received a call from an unknown number. An unknown voice on the other side said that my doctor friend that had rented the apartment for us sent his greetings and then promptly hung up. I got what that meant right away. Apparently, my friend was arrested and was warning us to relocate. We couldn't stay there any longer. I had attempted to cross the border a few more times, but because of my past experience, I changed my mind every time and couldn't do it. I was unhinged, doing things unintentionally, and I was constantly getting sick. My father couldn't take the stress anymore, and he had an angiography and bypass surgery. I couldn't even visit him. He needed blood, and I couldn't give him any of mine! I was so miserable!

No alternatives

There were only two options for me in Turkey, both of which terrified me; escape or return to prison. However, my previous escape attempt was so devastating that it prevented me from taking any steps forward. I summoned my courage by taking medication.

The smugglers took me again on a Saturday. There were two families and myself. I had heard and read a lot of stories. There were people who were robbed and murdered by smugglers; people who drowned in rivers; people who got caught; and even people who managed to escape only to get extradited back. Survival was never guaranteed, and anything could happen.

I was afraid, but I did not have any other option. I found myself near the river, trying to inflate a boat with people who had been suffering from the same fate as mine. My mind was lost amidst a torrent of horrible scenarios that could happen. What if soldiers showed up? What if the propeller of the boat did not work? Or what if the current was too strong? I was wracked with anxiety and stress the entire time.

Finally, we started our journey. Our boat was wobbling and hit the Turkish shore twice! Everybody was nervous and without hope. It was obvious that we would get caught without being able to complete the journey. A woman in our boat couldn't take the stress anymore and tried to jump into the river!

Greece

Finally, after a gruesome five-hour long journey, ten of us on the same boat managed to reach Greece. There were children among us. Can you imagine the terrifying experience they witnessed just in the beginning of their lives? Unfortunately, they also walked the upcoming five-hour walk, just like we did.

I was going to continue the journey with my friend. A friend of mine, who lives abroad, guided us by following us through cell phones. We tried to avoid the villages and the residential areas with his help. I cannot begin to describe how exhausted we were, but all I can say is that our shoes were torn into pieces from all of the walking.

Finally, we made it to a small city. After that, we decided to go to another city by bus but the police stopped our bus on the road. I was scared because in my last, unsuccessful attempt to flee, the smugglers had stamped a fake seal on my passport, and I would be sent back if the police recognized it. The police approached us and wanted to see our passports. Since we were fugitives, we were not walking around with our passports in our hands. We had hidden our passports in our socks, wrapped in plastic bags. They realized something was wrong after we took out our passports from where we hid them, feeling the eyes of everyone on us. The police told us to get out of the bus and started interrogating us. My friend immediately told them "We are running away from the President and his corrupt government!" The police officer was a bit angry, but he gave our passports back and told us to leave.

We were reborn. It was the first time we felt a bit of relief and realized that we had not eaten anything for a long time. First, we bought some tickets to travel onwards and then went to eat pizza. I began to think about my family, especially my father. He had just had heart surgery and we decided not to tell him about my journey in order to not work his heart up even more. I forgot about myself for a second and prayed to God for his health. I hoped that he was okay. I had a chance to say goodbye to only my wife and daughter. After a five to six-hour long journey, we reached another city and then continued on to Athens. We needed to stay there for two days. We found a two-room apartment where eight to nine refugees were staying and decided to stay there.

The US really is full of adventures

There is a popular Turkish song that goes, "America is full of adventures..." Our journey to the US would be full of adventures, indeed. When we arrived at the airport in Athens we were arrested because we had not entered Greece in normal ways. We were scared that we would not be able to fly to America, or worst of all, be extradited back to Turkey. But thank God, our fears did not come true.

We were on a plane that was headed to the US! In the end, we had struggled against so much adversity just for this moment. However, I did not experience happiness in that moment. I felt weary, sad, and lost. All I had known for the past few years was hardship and persecution. After everything I had been through, I felt like my sense of joy and happiness had been robbed from me.

After we set foot in the US we would be interrogated once again. They allowed me in only after I told them that I was not a dangerous person and that I had visited their country at least twenty times in the past.

My final destination

I've been in Canada now for only six months, and I am trying to build a new life for myself while being away from my family and loved ones. Despite these hardships, my only motivation to survive is my family. I came to this country without a penny in my pocket. I started sharing an apartment with a friend. A Turkish family sold me a car with a 9-month payment plan. Now, I deliver pizza with that car.

My wife delivered our second daughter after I arrived in Canada. Even though I cannot support my wife in her difficult days, and I don't get to experience the pleasure of holding my newborn daughter, we talk over the phone every day. Both of my daughters are growing up, and I have to watch these beauties from the other side of a phone. If you ask me the most meaningful thing I am doing in my life, I would say talking to my daughter over the phone at least three hours a day, no matter how tired I am.

I have applied for asylum and am waiting for the date of the hearing. I am trying to hang on to life both financially and emotionally. The climate and the living conditions here are very difficult. I am waiting for a miracle, even though I am not very hopeful. I hope to reunite with my family one day, improve my language skills so that I can work at a university here even if it is without pay. After all, life has given us things beyond our imagination, hasn't it? Why not this?

I have learned to find small sources of hope for survival throughout this journey, and to string these hopes together in order to ma ke a strong rope with which I cling to life.

4

A Breath

C.E.

"My lonely and beautiful country!"

There was once a poet, who, like me, had to flee his home country. He was labeled as a "traitor." "My lonely and beautiful country…" he lamented, voicing his pain. My lonely and beautiful country, and these words are what I keep in my heart nowadays.

You don't choose where you are born. Geography is a matter of fate, so "loneliness" became the fate for the "beautiful" people of Turkey for many generations.

Everyone has a story of loneliness. Mine, including a lot of people with the same fate, started on the 15th of July in 2016 in Turkey. Our fate was tied to a fake and bloody coup that took place on that day.

I was an instructor with a ninety-eight percent success rate at one of Istanbul's private universities. I was a dedicated faculty member and the university's administration assigned me a busy schedule for the upcoming year. Later, I would learn the hard truth of the bloody coup when I went to the university only to be informed by my department head that I had been dismissed from my position effective immediately. The administration, who had been telling me only a few weeks before that they had been planning to assign me to a busier schedule, did not even care to explain their decision. Their only response was, "We decided on it." Needless to say, I was left in a state of absolute shock and confusion.

Everyone was in a big state of panic. A sweeping witch hunt started shortly after the coup attempt even though the coup's details, such as the scope of the attempt or who its mastermind was, were largely unknown at the time. All of a sudden, ordinary people began to lose their jobs, were taken from their homes, and detained. An excuse, much like a state of emergency order with the name "OHAL," was fabricated for all of these illegal activities. No one was judging either the tortures or the detentions that continued for weeks.

As if that wasn't enough for my family and I, we would collapse when we found out that our son's school (Fatih Private Secondary School) had been shut down. Our nervousness increased when we could not find any answers when we went to the school to ask what would happen next. A terrible storm was heading right towards us and we had little to no time to prepare.

Burning holy books

We began to hear from our neighbors that anyone with some kind of ties to the Hizmet Movement were being targeted by the police. No one knew when the police would show up; perhaps today, tomorrow, or a week from now. The people who were blacklisted by the state as "Hizmet Movement Sympathizers" had to be prepared for the police, who were barging into homes in the middle of the night. Like many of our friends, we could not sleep for weeks. We usually stayed up late until the morning and told each other, "We should be presentable if they suddenly come to our home." Perhaps this was just an excuse for us since we were unable to sleep anyways. The stress and suspense were almost unbearable. As a result of being in a state of continuous nervousness and panic, we decided to move to a different address. In order not to face the same turmoil at our new home, we registered our address as if we lived in my wife's city.

Possessing certain books became a criminal offense as they served as "proof" of affiliation with the "Hizmet Terrorist Organization." We had several books that were now deemed to be illegal and decided that the best course of action would be to burn them.

We went to my father-in-law's place to burn the books there, even the Qur'an copies we had. While owning a Qur'an that was published by a pro-government company was okay, owning a Qur'an that was published by a Hizmet-affiliated company was a good enough reason to get arrested.

My younger son saw us burning the books in an earthenware jar and asked, in shock, "Mom? Dad? Why are you burning those books?"

How can one give a reasonable answer to such a question? My spouse and I just looked each other at a loss for words. We could only say, "We will explain this to you, but only when you get older... We promise."

Night raids

After a couple of months, we received a phone call from my wife's family. Because our residency was registered there, the police had raided their home and searched for hours. This would be the first of many raids.

My wife's family was so upset, and we were very anxious. Eventually, I made a decision. In order not to get them into more trouble, I went to the residency office and changed our address to a new one so that the police would no longer harass them.

My father-in-law used to be involved in political activities; he was known by many people with such a profile. More precisely, if we consider Hizmet Movement and AKP (the governing party) as two opposite poles, he was closer to the party side. As a result, he did not face many problems. Otherwise there have been many cases in which people to be detained and taken as hostages when the police were not able to find the family members that they really wanted. Their logic was simple; when you cannot find your suspect, then arrest a family member instead, until he or she turns themselves in.

As we learned there was an arrest warrant for us, we had to change our home one more time. I even had to use the ID of one of my relatives, who looked like me. He was aware of this of course, and we began to live at our new address with this new identity.

It was such an overwhelming time, and we were unfamiliar with our own selves. Everyone in the new neighborhood was trying to get to know who we were, where we worked, and where we came from. Entire communities were on edge, and people rapidly lost trust in their neighbors, friends, and even families. As we had to adopt new names for ourselves, we also had to make up a story to go along with them. We practiced our stories together at home. We were trying not to draw any attention to ourselves and had to be on the same page. It was becoming traumatic as time passed. When you make up stories, you sometimes mix up the details. Each one is a problem within itself.

These were the obstacles in our neighborhood, but our battle to survive in the larger society was also wearing us down. The government had declared a state of emergency, which was being reintroduced every three months. Police were doing searches everywhere, and this was enough a reason for anxiety. We were only going out when we needed to. We were constantly terrified. After all, I was carrying a fake ID, and that alone could suffice for us to be arrested. I could possibly go to jail without saying goodbye to my family.

One day, two friends and I were stuck at a police checkpoint. They asked for our IDs. There was no problem with my friend's, but the police got suspicious of mine. I was paralyzed with fear and my whole body began to shake. The policeman called other police at the checkpoint and asked for their opinions. They told me that we were going to go to the police station and investigate it there. I felt like I couldn't breathe. I was done. That was it! Everything was over. I was thinking of my family. As we were about to leave, one of the policemen asked me if I had another proof of ID on me. I showed my driver's license to him. After what seemed like an eternity, a higher-ranking officer said to let me go.

You can imagine how stressful everything was. The fact that my children had to be involved in this made me even more desperate. I am an experienced educator who specializes in special education. I was sadly becoming aware that the effects of the stress we were having were beginning to appear in my children. They were not being able to go out freely or enjoy themselves at a park or picnic as they felt the weight of our situation wearing them down. And perhaps more seriously, their mental health began to deteriorate due to constantly being stuck at home and under constant pressure.

We were afraid every time we heard a knock at the door. We even warned our kids to wait for us and to never open the door when someone knocked. One day, my older brother visited us and as he entered our home, my 2-year-old son told him that he did not make any noise and had waited for him quietly. My brother was speechless. We just looked into each other's eyes and became tearful. A child's uncle is visiting him, and instead of hugging him and yelling cheerfully he is aware that he needs to be quiet. Just before my eyes, my government was robbing my children of their innocence. Enough was enough. It was at that moment that I decided to leave my country.

When fathers disown their children

There was one reason I had not left the country until that moment. As it is known, many people lost their jobs as a result of government's executive orders, and most of them were jailed for ridiculous accusations. With no one to support them the families and relatives of these people were living under very difficult situations. I made it my responsibility to collect donations from charitable businessmen and other patrons in order to help those who were jobless or struggling because their loved ones were incarcerated. I was doing this secretly because helping victims of the government's persecution was a crime.

Women and children endured even worse conditions. Some women's husbands were in jail, some people were ostracized from society, and almost all of them were not even able to work even as a janitor because other people were blacklisting them as "terrorists." Can you imagine what it is like to have your world, your country, and your neighbors all turn on you in such a short span of time, and to lose your most basic human rights?

Circumstances became so bad that friends turned on each other seemingly overnight. Distrust and enmity became rampant throughout our communities, and people began to treat us like enemies even though we had done nothing wrong. This distrust caused some of our charitable donors to reject the people who were knocking on their doors because they were not able to determine whether they were real volunteers or police agents. Fortunately, since they had known me for a long time, I had gained their trust. What would happen if I was not there? Who would support these families?

Some may think, "perhaps you deserved this persecution." When you check the profiles of the people who support the Hizmet Movement, you will see that they are largely well-educated, law abiding, and contributing members of society. For instance, there was this college professor whose articles were published in many journals and had many patented inventions. He was arrested by the police and accused of being a member of "FETO," the so called "terrorist" organization name the government labeled Hizmet sympathizers with. (The term 'FETO' is a fabricated label by the Turkish government to categorize the sympathizers of Fethullah Gülen. It is a scare tactic serving multiple purposes; namely to generate division and implant fear in the eyes of the Turkish population as well as the rest of the world. President Recep Tayyip Erdoğan has thrown the name around for every problem in Turkey, much as how Hitler had blamed the Jews for everything. "FETO" is the ever serving scapegoat for an uprising dictator who is the real threat to a peaceful and successful Turkey.)

Individuals from almost all fields of expertise, ranging from education to media, science, medicine, law, etc. were being arrested. It was a huge brain drain from the country. You can say that most of the highly educated people of the country were either inside (in jail) or outside (had fled to other countries abroad). Could it ever be possible for so many highly educated people to lose their mind all at the same time to commit such enormous crimes, such as a coup, even though they had never committed a single crime before? I don't think this could be possible. Then the only other option we can make sense of this situation is that those who were accusing these people of being terrorists were possibly out of their minds. How can we otherwise explain this absurdity that considers supporting needy families as an act of terrorism?

A friend of mine, who was in a similar condition, was jailed. The "crime" that he had committed was being a sympathizer of the Hizmet Movement. His family did not even visit him because his father had disowned him. After a year, his family somehow convinced his father to change his mind. As the family was sitting in the waiting room, one of the prison guards approached him and asked if he was the father of my convicted friend. He shyly said that he was. Upon hearing the answer, the guard said to him, "Don't you have any shame? We have terrorists, killers, and robbers here, and even their families visit them. How come you are his father and disowned him? There is something called family ties!"

Another friend of mine had not been able to have a child for ten years. When his wife finally became pregnant, he got

detained. As a result, his wife gave birth when he was in prison. Her grandparents did not even visit her once and did not
provide any support either.

You can understand the level of insanity in my country
from these two examples. It has become a land where a Muslim shows no mercy to another Muslim, or a relative shows no
mercy to another relative. There is such a scary polarization
when a father disowns his child, a brother disowns his brother.

There are hundreds of these cases in my country.

Crossing the river

By now, we knew that we had to flee Turkey, but did not know
how. There was an arrest warrant for me and I would be detained the minute I got to the airport. We had to find another way to escape the country. I had questions in my mind:
Should I take my family with me, or leave them behind? What
if something happens to them while I am away? How can I live
with such a regret? What happens to the needy families when
I am gone? Am I putting my own kids at risk, am I causing
them to suffer while I am trying to help other victims?

I was lost in these thoughts. One day I went to talk with
someone who would help me escape. It was Friday, and he gave
me options for the departure day. I had to go as soon as I could.
So I chose to go that coming Sunday, which was also my wife's
birthday. I wanted to give her the gift of all; escaping this open-
air prison, and the relief of freedom for her and our children.

We hit the road without much preparation. We met our
fellow travelers at the point that the smuggler's had designated
for us. A former military officer who was dismissed from the
army was also there with his wife and two kids trying to es-

cape. We were able to reach a town close to the Maritsa River at noon. The smugglers left us in a nearby forest and told us to wait there until they would take us when it became dark. We did not have a chance to ask our friends who made this journey before, so we were naively expecting to stay at least in a tent or a cottage. None of them; it was an open area in the forest where we were told to wait. And we did so when all of a sudden it started to rain.

It rained continuously for 7-8 hours, and we just waited helplessly, completely soaked. We had little to no time to prepare, and had not considered all the possibilities. Unfortunately, we figured out after some hours that we could get some protection from the rain by using the plastic bags in our luggage. In the February cold, we felt as if even our bones were wet.

I will never forget watching my older son sitting without motion under a plastic bag. I snuggled him to me, and asked if he was okay. He did not make any sound and sat as if paralyzed. We became very worried about him.

Before setting off for the journey, my wife and I had concocted a story to tell the kids in order to not cause them to panic excessively or worry. We told them that we were going on a safari and it was going to be very adventurous. It was my son's dream to go on a safari with me. I told him that we were going to pass through mud and rivers as a "pre-safari" test, and then, if we could pass it, there would be a real one when he turned 15. My poor son was apparently trying to stay strong and not give up. However, to see him motionless shook us to our cores.

After endless hours in the dark, two smugglers finally came to meet us. They told us that we would be leaving and wanted us to leave some of our luggage behind since there was too much weight. Thus, I had to leave the luggage that contained the clothing for my son and myself. I put my essentials in my backpack, picked up my younger son, and we hit the road. I had not even taken a couple of steps when I slipped in the mud and fell on my back. I was hurt and panicked. My son began to cry loudly in fear. It was completely dark and even the smallest noise echoed through the forest. The smugglers were continuously warning us to be quiet since there were soldiers patrolling nearby, hunting for "terrorists" such as us. I begged him not to cry and told him we don't want "them" to hear us. My poor child sighed and began to quiet down. Normally, my kids are grumpy, but they were aware something different was happening so they were quiet that night. For four hours, we had to walk in the mud. It was raining continuously and everywhere became a swamp. We were buried in mud up to our kneecaps and were barely proceeding.

Sacrifice

Finally, after what seemed like an endless march through the night, we arrived at the border of the Maritsa River. It was finally going to happen; we were about to pass the river. As we were waiting in excitement, one of the smugglers told us to wait there some more as they were going to check around. They stated that there was a point which they could survey the river from a very good angle, and they needed to make sure that the area was safe. They told us they would be back in 15 minutes and left.

Time was passing, our anxiety was quickly rising, and our guides were not showing up. "We are deceived," we thought. We were thinking about what to do in the cold weather at that time of the night, but then they came back. They told us that we had to wait there for 7-8 more hours. The gendarmerie (military police) were patrolling the border of the river, and it was risky to move at that moment. But it was comparable to death to stay in those conditions any longer. I took a look around and thought to myself about other possibilities. The weather was extremely cold and we were soaking wet, fatigued, hungry, and barely even had the strength left to walk, and most importantly, my children were shaking terribly.

Yes, I started this trip for freedom, but I would not forgive myself if something happened to my kids. I made a very hard decision and told the smugglers that I would report myself because my sons would not be able to withstand these conditions. I told them that I would switch on my phone and turn myself in. I would be arrested, but my children would be saved.

I apologized to my fellow travelers for leaving them in the middle of the journey. They were more prepared for the trip and could continue to stay there. I told them they could go farther, and then I would call the gendarmerie.

I was about to turn on my phone, and then one of the smugglers immediately called their boss in panic and told him, "He will do something crazy and expose all of us!"

The voice on the other side of the phone call ordered the smugglers to take us across the river at all costs. At that moment, there was another patrolling vehicle, and we jumped into the mud in panic.

Floating upon death

The smugglers had a rafting boat with them and were inflating it. One of the guides went back to eliminate some of the evidence that we had left behind. We were going to cross the river with another person. I had simple life vests with me for my kids. I was so overwhelmed with panic and fear in that moment that I could not make my kids put them on, so I threw them away!

Everything was happening in seconds. We pushed the boat into the river, and nine people (four children and one smuggler among them) got on it. We were kneeling, and as we did, we got buried in water up to our belly. We quickly realized that our worst fears were coming true, and that the boat was losing air! I had warned them about this in the beginning, but they disregarded my warnings. In just a few second we found ourselves moving in the river in that boat.

A deflating boat, extremely cold weather, patrolling gendarmerie, and water that was reaching our bellies. Everything was against us; and all apparent means and causes were of no help. We had covered only a short distance into the river when the boat began to spin around. There was a scary stream current due to the heavy rain which had not stopped the whole day. The river was flowing high, and it was cold winter. I felt such a regret that I had risked my family's life to attempt such a dangerous journey. I questioned my reasoning throughout the night and doubted myself repeatedly. I thought that I shouldn't have done this even if I had to spend my life in jail. But still, we went onwards.

Watching what was happening was like being in a scary movie. I was thinking of everything that could go wrong in a matter of seconds. What if the boat sinks? How could I save them? How could I swim in this current? I remembered the woman who lost her husband and kids when they were try-

ing to cross the Maritsa River. Her husband and kids disappeared in the river, and she was the only one who could reach
the coast.

Most likely, this would end up being a day like hers. There
was a strong current and it was not possible to control the boat
as the water around us kept swirling. I felt that death was so
close to us. I was sure that we were at the end of everything and
that our boat was going to sink right there. My fellow travelers
were all hugging their kids and submitting themselves to the
Creator, saying their final prayers and accepting that their time
had come. My little son was awake in my wife's lap and crying,
"Mom! My feet hurt! Please, let's get out of the boat!" I took a
look at my wife who was helplessly trying to quiet him down.
The boat was spinning around out of control and was deflating.
I was blaming myself and thinking that I did not have the right
to do this to them.

I don't remember how long the trip took, but I can only
recall that finally the boat came close to a rocky shore alongside which we were drifting. At that moment, the army officer
friend stood up and fell off the boat. Thank God he was able to
grasp a branch as he fell. If he had tried to hold on to the boat
instead, I would not be able to narrate our story now.

I was the one who landed first. While I was climbing the
rocks, the guide was holding the boat tight and in order for
the boat not to move, the others were holding the bushes. As I
went higher, I fixed my feet somewhere and with my head upside down, I tried to help the others climb out. I pulled the kids
out first, then the women, and the army officer last.

It felt like centuries. Suddenly, everybody looked each other and began to cry with the relief of escaping. Was it really

Greece? "Yes," said the guide. "You are in Greece!" Thank God, we had escaped!

Russian roulette

We had somehow survived, but the same boat was going to be a coffin for other refugees only five days later. They made an agreement with the same smugglers that we did, chose to take that nerve-breaking trip, and as they got on the boat, they noticed it was deflating and began to pray to survive. However, they did not make it. For us, not to be in their shoes was God's choice.

We could not even breathe when we heard the horrific news. My wife cried for days, read the news again, and cried over and over. There was only one person who survived, and the story he told was exactly the same as ours. God wanted them to be martyrs, but we were in agony from their tragedy.

For many days my wife and I pondered over all that happened during our escape. "Would we do this if we knew what was going to happen?" The answer was no. It was impossible for us to think of doing the same journey again, even if we knew that we were going to escape in the end.

After that tragic river trip, we landed in Greece, and walked without a break for hours. Similar to our journey on the way to the Maritsa River, we walked hungry and thirsty in the mud for four hours. We were tired, had a big load, and were constantly slowed down by the swamp. In the pitch-black, we were not even able to see each other. We would not realize that we were covered in mud until the daybreak. Our jaws were shaking from the cold weather. The children were the same. Their shoes and socks were completely wet. We attempted to take their socks from their backpacks, but they were wet too. As a last resort, we took off our gloves and put them on the children's feet as socks.

Not all heroes are giants

We were exhausted from walking and were about to give up. My wife had no strength left from tromping in the mud. Like a miracle, my 6-year-old son was walking at the same pace with us. It was absolutely astounding that that little body was walking without any complaints. His courage and resolution were absolutely inspiring in such a dire moment. For a moment, I took my younger child in my arms and moved ahead. Our army officer friend and his wife were close to us as well.

I was to learn later that my wife was about to collapse. But my precious son told her, "Mom, let's catch dad! They passed ahead of us!" and did not let her give up. Afterwards, we would call him our "Hero." With the help of God, he motivated his mom, and all of us, even when his shoes were torn and his feet injured, which I would learn much later. But he did not complain and continued walking.

God, it was such a long night! It was still not over after so much had happened to us already. Around 4 a.m. we finally arrived at a village but had no idea what to do next. There was nobody around. We saw an old train station and went in there to change our muddy clothes with damp but at least clean clothes.

The cold weather got even colder at that time of the night. We were all faced with the risk of becoming frozen, especially the kids. Our endurance was coming to a level of exhaustion. We discussed our situation with the other friends, and as a last resort, we decided to knock on the doors of the homes in the village. Of course, nobody opened their doors at that time of the night.

We were helpless and weak. There were no people or cars anywhere, and we were losing our hopes. But we did not have the luxury of giving up. We at least could not give up for the kids. With little hope, we continued walking among the homes, and finally, one of the doors cracked open. It was a woman who looked at us and made a gesture as if to say, "Wait!" She came back with a man who we realized was her husband. I apologized and tried to explain them that we were coming from Turkey. I said that we were about to freeze. I begged them for help. Thankfully, Mr. Dimitri were familiar with some Turkish vocabulary, and he was able to understand our situation.

If my son was the first hero of this difficult trip, Mr. and Mrs. Dimitri were the second; they accepted people they did not know and saved them from freezing at that time of the night. They took us to the basement of their house which he was using as a repair room. There were two coal stoves, and Mr. Dimitri lit them quickly. While he was serving tea and coffee to us, his wife brought milk and toast. These two beautiful people woke from their sleep and served us at night. Their presence was surely a divine grace for us.

We Turkish people, unfortunately, are often raised with hostility towards the Greek people. In our narrow minds, we are taught to consider them as traitors, evil people, and invaders; this was how we were taught at school. God helped us get rid of those ridiculous prejudices by allowing us to meet Mr. Dimitri and his wife at their home. Not only that night, but also many other days, we were going to witness the same kindness and hospitality of the Greek people. We always proclaim that the Turkish people are the most hospitable people in the world, but we would find out that those Greek people were better than us.

Uncle Dimitri did not go to bed again and he stayed up with us until 8 am in the morning. The others took a nap, but I was not able to sleep at all. He kept me company while he was trying to find solutions for us. He really wanted to help us, but it was forbidden to help illegal immigrants or smugglers according to Greek laws. He said he was okay with us staying at his home, but he could not help us if we went out of his home. He decided to direct us to one of his friend's hotels in a nearby town where we could take a shower and have a rest before we surrendered to the police. One of my fellow travelers did not have a passport and was afraid of not being accepted at the hotel. Uncle Dimitri ensured us that he would talk with his friend at the hotel. Thanks to his support, my fellow travelers had no trouble being accepted at the hotel.

After that horrific night, the hotel was like heaven for us. We took a shower, cleaned up, and were able to sleep in peace. We had the opportunity to think straight. We were going to surrender to the police in Athens. We had heard from friends that if we surrendered in Athens we would not need to stay in the refugee camp.

We decided to take our chance on going to Athens and left the hotel. While we were buying our tickets, the ladies were shopping for the kids' needs in a shopping center. We did not know that there was a police station just by the shopping center. The police noticed the kids and asked for their IDs. My wife called me in panic, and as a result of her panic, I called some friends and asked them what to do. They calmed me down and told us to buy blankets, water, food, and to surrender to the police. Eventually, we were going to surrender to the police anyway.

After we bought the suggested things the police transferred us in a van to a police station. After being held for 24 hours and having our fingerprints taken, we were taken to a refugee camp. There were many people with different nationalities. It felt like everyone in the world was brought together in that place.

The refugee camp

I am not exaggerating, but if we did not know we were in Greece we would not believe it was, for the camp looked like a prison in Yemen or at Guantanamo Bay, or other places with notoriety in the media. There was no torture, but when you consider the conditions, it was no different. The sewer was leaking inside, and everywhere was full of dirt. We were breathing the same air with hundreds of people and it smelled extremely bad. Plus, it was almost impossible to breath because of the heavy cigarette smoke. I am sure that an average person couldn't imagine such a disgusting place in his whole life!

As we entered and looked around with fearful eyes, a teenager approached us. He was a 17-year-old boy from Şanlıurfa, Turkey, who was sentenced to jail for being a "terrorist" and had to flee from his country. He had been there for the last two weeks. He felt the need to approach and help us, as he had noticed our sullen faces. I guessed he was used to the camp since he had been there for a while. He immediately went to the back of the room and got two bunk beds emptied and surrounded them with dirty blankets for us. We were able to have some privacy like that. So we were – partially – isolated from our surroundings. We also laid out our new blankets and the place became as pleasant as it could possibly be under such conditions. The young man spoke to us in a comforting manner; "Don't worry," he said, "they keep the Turks here for a day at most." He stayed in the camp longer because he was involved in a ship smuggling.

It was as if God had kept that young man waiting for all those days to help us, because only an hour after we met and he helped us they took him out from the camp. And just as he said, exactly 24 hours later, our names were announced and we were given our papers.

After we left the camp, we stayed in a hotel one more day and then made a transit pass to Athens from Thessaloniki. As a result, we had to go in different directions from our fellow travelers. We wished success to each other and moved to our friends in Athens.

We had the opportunity to have a stay there awhile and think things over. We did not have any intention of settling in Greece. We took the trip in the first place with the intention of going to the USA or Canada. Therefore, we did not need to stay in Greece long and get used to the conditions. But we had a problem: we could not afford the tickets to the USA. Besides it would not be easy to leave Greece for we have not entered it legally. As a result, we decided to move to Georgia. Tickets to Georgia were cheap, and also we wanted to prove to ourselves that if we could go there that we could go anywhere else in the world.

We were very anxious as we entered the airport. The official who took our passports asked us to wait and left. In a while, he came back and told us "You are free to go, but why Georgia?"

What he meant with that question was "I know why you are here. So, why not a more democratic country?"

Since the very first minute that we had entered Greece, everybody, including the officer in the airport, treated us as welcoming as possible. However, we did not have another option.

The fear of deportation

We were relieved as we did not face any problems when entering Georgia. We were going to face the real challenges – and understand what the Greek officer meant – when we tried to leave from there.

While in Georgia, I heard that visitors could stay up to ninety days in a South American country. This would allow us some time and make plans for our future. So, we purchased tickets which had a few stopovers. We had to use two different airline companies.

When we went to the airport to leave Georgia, the immigration officer who could speak some Turkish checked the passports of my children and stated that there were no stamps of departure from Turkey, and therefore he would not allow us to board. I objected and told him that we had been able to come to their country legally, and they had accepted us. I argued with him, but he did not listen to me. He was very grumpy and told us that he would deport us and did not care what we would face back in Turkey. We were scared to death, but he was not listening to any of our objections. He was going to send us back to Turkey on the 4:30 flight.

God, did we have to endure all of this only to end up going back to Turkey? We were paralyzed and did not know what to do. We were not able to argue with him. He somehow got suspicious; maybe we did not really look like people who would fly to Colombia. He abruptly said, "You are escaping from Erdoğan, and I will not let this happen!" I tried to stay calm and speak with him in English. He was speaking in Turkish with me, and his English was not good. I said, "My Turkish is not so well, but we are not escaping from Erdogan."

His supervisor noticed the situation and came over. I was trying to express myself to him as well, but the other officer was interfering and trying to bring him to his side. The supervisor told us to wait and left with the other officer. We were able to see that they were checking our passports. He called some other officers and used a magnifying glass to check the passports. We noticed that the Greeks did another favor for us. They stamped the other people's passports as "Fugitive" but did not do this on our passports. Thus, there was only the regular departure stamp.

My patience was fading away as their checking took longer and longer, and the flight time was coming very soon. I quickly approached them, and told them that our plane was about to take off, and we did not have any money left to buy extra tickets. I requested they let us go. The supervisor told me that he was holding the plane, and it would take off after they made a decision about us. Or they would just send us back to Turkey.

At that moment I was not able to figure out whether he was bluffing or not, but we learned in the next few minutes that he was telling the truth. With only a few minutes left before the airplane would take off, he approached us and said, "Okay, you are allowed to go." I could hardly contain myself not to scream with cheer. We had to look calm. At the very last minute, they stamped our passports and we got on the plane.

"We have to ask Interpol about you!"

We were transit passengers, so we had to pass through many security checks in several different airports.

In some of those places they took our passports and stirred up trouble. In one occasion, when the officials told us they had to consult Interpol, we began to panic. We were living the same nightmare over and over again. Once again, they took our passports and left. We were not able to communicate with them properly, we did not have internet connection, and there was nobody who could tell us what to do. We were only waiting helplessly, lost in a country that we had no familiarity with, for what was coming next.

We were under a lot of stress. Looking at the airport's terrible conditions, we could not even imagine how horrific the prison would be. We knew we would either go to jail or be deported if they did not let us leave from there. We were caught between two fires.

As time passed, we became more and more nervous. In addition, we were trying to hide our stress from the kids. They were running, playing games cheerfully, and my younger son was acting like a cheerleader. My older son was asking me to play games with him. They were comfortable in their innocent world while we were scared to death. My wife and I were looking at each other's faces and were overrun with anxiety since we did not know what was ahead of us.

All of a sudden, I remembered that my Turkish phone line

still had some data to make a call for a couple of minutes; so I called one of my friends immediately. He relieved my fears and told me that we would not face any problems if we had not previously caused any trouble with Interpol. He ensured me that in the worst case scenario, they would tell us that they would deport us, and we could seek asylum. I felt much better after talking with him. A few more officers came to check our passports and tickets. Finally, we were allowed to move on. We hardly made it before the doors to the plane were closed.

When we arrived in our last stop on this journey we had already been conditioned to always expect the worst.

After those hard days of traveling, we stayed in one of my friend's home for 10 days. Then we moved to a furnished rental apartment. We were not planning to stay there long but needed to make a plan. My plan was to start a company in my wife's name and get a US or Canadian visa for my family; I had a visa to the US, but my family did not. We founded the company in my wife's name, and they gave us three-year residency in this South American country. This was such a relief for us, as we finally felt that we could settle somewhere, at least temporarily, and not be constantly homeless and on the run. Then I began to have another fear when I was about to apply for a visa for my family: What if my visa was canceled? Even though I did not know the reasons, I was aware that some of my friends' visas had been canceled. Luckily, I had a short trip to the US and saw that there was no trouble.

I had time to think over everything while I was flying back. Recently, it had become difficult to get an American visa, and I did not know if I would be able to get one for my family. On the other hand, we did not have the financial conditions or a job which would allow us stay in this country for a long period of time. In addition, my older son had to start school. Therefore, we needed to make a decision and settle down.

It had been almost two and a half months since we had left Turkey. We had become nomads and this uncertainty began to get really tiresome. As a last resort, we decided to go to America through Mexico. I was going to use the regular ways to get there, but my family was going to try to cross the border. We were totally aware that this was very risky but we felt we had no other choice. Eventually, we bought tickets and went to Mexico which was our fifth stop on our journey from Turkey.

Mexico

One might have thought of us as a happy family who had come to Mexico City as tourists. But on the contrary, there was a storm breaking in our hearts. Having stayed in a hotel in Mexico City, we then went to Tijuana and stayed in a hotel there. My intention was to explore the Mexican border with my wife.

We had a funny moment in Tijuana which I would like to mention. We understood later that the cab driver had dropped us off in the car transit area on the border. As we were looking around to find out where we have arrived, a man suddenly showed up. Not just showing up, but literally sticking to us, and began to ask questions. "Are you going to US? Why are you looking around?" He was a strange guy who had some Spanish writing on his clothes. Was he an undercover police officer? We panicked one more time and thought we had finally got caught. We had overcome so many obstacles, interrogations, and had escaped from many dangers. We told the guy that we were tourists coming from Mexico City and were looking for our hotel. It turned out that he was a scammer who was trying to steal money from tourists. We would not even understand what was happening, but he called a cab and ordered the cab driver to take us back to our hotel.

We entered the hotel, made the necessary preparations, and went out to do our exploration in a better way. That time we checked online and looked at the pictures, which led us to the correct location to observe the border better. We hung around like tourists and took some pictures. We collected some memories which we will hopefully remember as good moments to tell our grandchildren about after facing so much anxiety.

My wife and I sat and had a detailed conversation. It was certain that we could not stay there long and had to somehow get to the US. The most practical solution for my family was to cross the Mexican border and seek asylum afterwards. As a part of the plan, since I had a visa, I took the first flight and went to Houston. Right after I landed, I called my wife and told her to take action immediately.

I was so stressed and full of anxiety for them to accomplish this adventurous task. I had finished my part of the journey, but my wife and children had yet to finish theirs. I would like my wife to share her side of this story since I was not there to narrate my perspective.

So close to freedom, yet so far
(Narration from my wife)

As my husband flew to Houston, we had to stay in the hotel one more night. As you can guess, I stayed up the whole night. I was extremely stressed. What was next? What was waiting for us? What would I do with my very limited English, and how could I cross the border with two kids? We checked out of the hotel and took a cab that the hotel worker had called for us. I told the driver "border" but was concerned with the possibility that he could take us somewhere else. Thankfully, he took us to the right place.

As we got out of the cab, we began to walk at a quick pace. I was so afraid of the possibility that someone could realize my plan because of my state of panic. I was holding my suitcase in one hand and the kids in the other one. All of a sudden, I took a look around me and noticed that everybody was walking at the same pace. I was moving fast because of my fear, but they were doing this to be able to move ahead in the line. I did not want to draw attention like that. It was like an endless marathon to the gate.

What we called "the gate" was a simple border gate for daily usage. It was open, and no police were watching it. Nobody asked us where we were going even though it was the initial point to enter the US. But after that point, you needed to submit your documents, and there were not only refugees but tourists as well.

We saw an available spot and immediately got in line there. When it was our turn the police officer asked for my passport I could only say, "I want asylum." Per my statement they took us to a side room. In that room, four people, whom I believed to be African, were also waiting. Although I would be able to be there with my kids, I was extremely anxious. I could not help that my hands and feet were shaking. Yet, I texted my husband and informed him that we were in America. I was going to learn later that as he was waiting he thought we were in the wrong place and even had a short panic attack. He thought we got caught by the police inside Mexico and burst into tears since he thought we would never be able to see each other again. After such a long and difficult journey, this possibility was really disturbing.

After waiting for a couple of hours, a crowded group of policemen came for us. The ones who were seeking asylum formed a separate line. They had us take off all our accessories like hats, hair pins, belts, shoe laces, etc. and began to take us one by one for an interview.

We were asked many questions such as, "Do you have any diseases? Where are you coming from? Why are you here? Why do you seek asylum?" I spoke honestly and said that I was a member of the Hizmet Movement, and that there was an arrest warrant for my husband in Turkey. They were surprised about my statement and repeated the question again. I said the same thing and told them that we were victimized by the Erdogan government.

After we completed our interview, we began to wait. The others also had to complete their interview. I only became aware that there was a long line at that moment. There were a lot of official procedures to be done. They took our passports, fingerprinted us, and took us to a big hall. It was like a gym which had no chairs but some cushions on the floor and bathrooms on the sides. In the next few hours, we were going to share the hall with approximately 60 people. It was such a huge crowd. There were two mats for my kids and myself to sleep on, and which I had to share lying back to back with a woman whom I did not know.

Most probably, in order not to let germs increase in the heat, the AC was made to be very cold, which ironically began to make my kids sick. We had never faced any bad treatment though, and felt at relative peace. Everybody was doing their job calmly. They were serving food in short periods, but much of the food was not permissible according to our dietary restrictions. It was mostly ham and non-halal chicken. We had no choice but to eat the bread when we got really hungry. The conditions were tough, and not knowing how long it would take was making it even harder.

Locked up in a tiny, extremely cold, unsanitary, and crowded place, unable to contact my husband or anyone else, and lost sense of time (there was no clock anywhere), it was so hard for me to endure these conditions. We were aware that they could not deport us without the judicial decision, but it was difficult to wait. The families we talked with before told us that we would stay there for a few days, but time was passing by and our hope was decreasing with every passing day.

I was okay, but I needed to keep the kids busy. We prayed to God together every day. Even my little son was praying over and over, asking him to let us go to his dad. I was teaching them some short prayers like "Subhanallah" ("Glory be to God"). My older one said that prayer thousands of times every day. There was nothing else to do but play games and say prayers.

We naturally had a lot of time to think. I was thinking to myself, "I cannot even stand waiting here for a couple of days, but my friends in Turkey were in jail for years and for no reason. How could they stand it?" It would be unbearable for anyone in those conditions. I felt their agony. This was painful to imagine, but it also helped me to be more patient. It made me not feel the pain of being locked up when I was expecting to be free. Actually, this was an opportunity for me to be able to share a small part of my friends' sorrow. I would never forget them in my prayers. I asked God to help them and end all the cruelty of my people.

We only stayed there for five nights, and I really tried hard to keep my kids happy. We were playing games, solving math questions, and having conversations. But, my mind kept drift and I continuously wondered about the mothers who were in jails with their babies in Turkey. How could they stay in such horrendous conditions with little babies who needed care and love all the time?

The other people in the hall were not paying attention to us. They were mostly killing time by eating and sleeping. Sometimes their attention was drawn to us while we were playing games, chatting, and making cars and airplanes with papers. My younger one, being just a little child, was playing games and not aware that he had become the source of joy for everyone there.

Finally, after five long days our prison-like days ended. It was the 30th of April and it was an important Muslim holiday: the fifteenth of Shaban, or the night of Baraa, which literally meant "acquittal." We felt reborn again and thanked God for saving us.

Free at last

It was amazing to reach my husband after an exhausting wait with my kids for five days. We were planning to settle in the US, but I began to have different thoughts in the next few days and wondered if we should go to Canada instead. Canada was one of the options in my mind when we were leaving Turkey. After overcoming so many obstacles, why not? Canada seemed more appealing to us because the asylum process was faster, and the conditions were better for us there.

After some discussion, we decided to stay in the US because we had no energy left to have another adventurous border crossing. After such a hard time, we really needed a peaceful and ordinary life. Eventually we submitted ourselves to God and decided to stay in the US.

Crossing the Maritsa River was when we felt on the edge between life and death. We then were so scared of being deported during the interrogations when they confiscated our passports. Now, a new life was waiting for us after all we had faced. We consider our new home as an opportunity like a window to freedom, innovation, and the free world. We endured all this agony for our kids rather than ourselves. Our only wish is that they will never ever forget why we had to stand up against all these problems.